Frantic Semantics

JOHN MORRISH

Frantic Semantics

Snapshots of our Changing Language

MACMILLAN

First published 1999 by Macmillan
an imprint of Macmillan Publishers Ltd
25 Eccleston Place, London SW1W 9NF
Basingstoke and Oxford
Associated companies throughout the world
www.macmillan.co.uk

ISBN 0 333 76352 1

3 5 7 9 8 6 4

A CIP catalogue record for this book is available from
the British Library.

Typeset by SetSystems Ltd, Saffron Walden, Essex
Printed and bound in Great Britain by
Mackays of Chatham plc, Chatham, Kent

*For my mother and father, who first
helped me find the right words*

Frantic Semantics

" The editor will see you now "

FOREWORD

Words are slippery. They change the way they sound, the way they look, the way they behave. And they change their meanings – their semantics – sometimes in a way that is wild, uncontrolled, even frantic.

The snapshots that follow aim to document words as they are used today. But they are also snapshots in an earlier sense: that of letting fly with a gun at something that has suddenly jumped up in front of you. Then, of course, you have to go and take a look, to see exactly what you've shot.

With words, it's not that easy. You can't shoot them, or photograph them, and they don't lie still while you examine them. Moreover, there's limited agreement about where they come from and what they mean.

The words captured on these pages are mostly still in use, on the television and radio, in newspapers and magazines, in conversations overheard in the street. They were chosen because they were interesting, rather than because they were particularly new.

So if you need to know what a 'car-bra' is, you'll need a different book. Such 'neologisms', used by almost no one, are the lifeblood of modern dictionaries. But they have less to tell us than the words we use every day, sometimes without being sure what they mean.

The temptation to say 'what they really mean' is very strong. I am very grateful to readers of the *Telegraph* magazine, where versions of these pieces first appeared, for contributing so many interesting words over the years. Often the 'real' meaning is what they are looking for.

Sadly, this sort of loose talk drives academics into despair. Even the broad-minded David Crystal, doyen of English language studies, devotes a couple of paragraphs in his marvellous *Cambridge Encyclopaedia of the English Language* to attacking the 'etymological fallacy': the idea that an earlier meaning of a word is the 'real' one.

'The sense of a modern lexeme [a word] depends on the way it is used now, and not on its semantic antecedents, which are often multiple and obscure,' he says. 'Fascinating as etymologies are, in debate they can only be a rhetorical cheat.'

This is true. There's nothing worse than a speech or an article that uses a perverse dictionary definition as the starting point for a ringing condemnation or a string of jokes. One day, I will stop doing it. In the meantime, I shall watch my language. Perhaps the Elizabethan, or Victorian, or original Greenland Eskimo meaning of a word is not its 'real' meaning.

Nonetheless, we can all take pleasure in the fact that the estate agents' favourite adjective, 'prestigious', once meant 'untrustworthy', and that 'glamour' was once a technique in witchcraft. The point about the Frantic Semantics is that they are supposed to be fun. Accurate, usually: comprehensive and balanced, occasionally; entertaining, wherever possible. From the tangled etymological pathways leading to our modern word, I have tended to choose the scenic route.

I notice, reworking these items, that they constitute in passing a portrait not only of individual words, but of an era. We have all travelled a long way in the last few years, from 'warm beer' to Cool Britannia and beyond; through a global revolution in electronics and communication; through a battering period for ancient institutions; through unparalleled American cultural dominance; through the beginning of a European union, with us or without us.

Our desire to find the 'real' meaning of a word is not negligible. We are not fools: we know that words don't mean what they meant sixty or six hundred years ago. And yet, it is my belief (and I apologize if it sounds mystical) that words contain within themselves their previous lives. We hear in them not only the way we use them now, but also the way our parents used them, and their parents before them.

Those previous lives are important. In the past, people thought words were like currency. They were coined, passed from hand to hand and worn down, devalued or adulterated. It is a seductive analogy, but today we have wider sources for our metaphors.

Words are like living things, but simple ones. No one coins or manufactures them, they just come into being, in response to a need. If we keep them moving, they live indefinitely, do various useful tasks, even do great harm. As they move around, they change. They get shorter or longer. They take on more tasks. Sometimes two words try to do the same job, and then the fittest, the most usable, survives. Sometimes they take on too much, become overstretched and unreliable. Or the function they embody disappears, in which case they don't exactly die, but go for a quiet lie-down in the offices of the Oxford University Press.

Rather like a virus, but with fewer symptoms, a word is nothing but information. English spelling and pronunciation, though baffling and illogical for those learning the language, are part of that information. They tell us where the word came from, how it relates to other words and what it's likely to mean.

We learn a word's connotations, the associations it carries beyond the dictionary 'meaning', by hearing it in context, from childhood or from the appearance of the word. Which is why, if you will forgive the sudden change of metaphor, a word has resonances. Say it out loud and, like a note struck on a grand piano, it rings, producing innumerable resonances and associations. If we listen carefully, we can hear them.

That may be why we react badly to some words without knowing why. Often the reasons are obvious. People don't like 'partner' because it's prissy, smug and mealy-mouthed. They don't like 'tad' because it's American. But why don't they like 'customer'? Because it sounds insincere. When we go to Shakespeare, and discover that he used it to mean 'whore', things become clear. Within the complex timbre of many English words can be heard an insistent sexual note.

It would be nice to claim that *Frantic Semantics* was the product of a lifetime's scholarship in the dust-laden stacks of a great university library, where I labour over noun compounds in *The Battle of Maldon*, emerging occasionally to pen three hundred words on 'blag'. This would not be true. I am an amateur, in the real sense of the word (oops, there I go again) but I do what I can, making use of the accumulated expertise of the scholars and trying not to falsify what they have to say in my unending search for a punchline.

It might help to have a brief outline of the development of English. Thousands of years ago, and this is a conjecture, there seems to have been a common language among the inhabitants of central Europe. This Proto-Indo-European broke into innumerable languages as those who first spoke it spread across the continent. In the north of Europe, a variant now called Germanic came into being. That in turn split into numerous languages, among them the tongues of the Angles, Saxons, Frisians and Jutes.

At the beginning of the fifth century AD, Celts occupied England and Wales, as subjects of the Romans, whose bricklaying skills had kept the Scots and Picts at bay. Unfortunately, the Romans had trouble at home, so the Celts sought the help of a few tentative Saxons, Angles and Jutes, who came over to eastern England from what is now north Germany and Denmark. Then the newcomers invited the rest of the family and a few friends, despatching the Celts to Wales, where they have been ever since.

Few traces of either Celtic or Roman Latin remain in English, except in place names. The newcomers spoke their own variants on Germanic, which evolved together into what they called Englisc. We call it Old English, and call them the Anglo-Saxons. They wrote, what little they did write, in 'runes', the mysterious stick-writing beloved of 1970s heavy metal bands. Then at the end of the sixth century, they started to be converted to Christianity, and were taught to write.

Unfortunately, very little Old English writing survives: the entire body of work amounts to only about 3.5 million words, fewer than are contained in the fiction rack at your local petrol station. In *Frantic Semantics*, there are frequent references to Old English words appearing around the year AD 1000: but that relates only to the date of the surviving texts. The words might be five hundred years older.

From the end of the eighth century, England was invaded by the Vikings, another Germanic tribe with another language, called Old Norse. They held half the country, leaving a lasting mark on English but probably destroying many of its texts. And then William the Conqueror arrived, in 1066.

After that, things settled down, at least once the Anglo-Saxons started to pick up some Norman French, and the Normans decided they didn't mind their children using the Englisc language. This period, from about the middle of the twelfth century, gave us Middle English. From there to modern English is a smoother transition, marked more by the working out of competing influences rather than bloodcurdling contests on the battlefield. By the time of Shakespeare and the King James Bible, the language looks quite like our own: the centrality of those texts has been a factor in maintaining that continuity almost to the present day.

Since then, the English, accompanied by the Scots, Welsh and Irish at various times, have roamed the world. Among the booty they brought back were words from numerous other languages. What's more, they left their own language out there, where it has continued to develop and evolve in its own way. It is appealing to think that English is uniquely fitted, through its 'simplicity', to be a world lingua franca. The truth is that it owes that role to two historical factors: the British Empire and the American Empire.

For those who want more scholarly information, or who would just like to pursue some of the lines of inquiry opened up by *Frantic Semantics*, there are plenty of places to look. In the first place, the book would have been impossible without the *Oxford English Dictionary*, the invariable starting point for my inquiries: when no source is mentioned for etymological material, it will almost invariably be the *OED*. More than a wonderful book (or books), it's one of the great achievements of British civilization. By modern lexicographical standards it is unreliable, idiosyncratic and biased towards the canon of great authors, but if I ever end up on a desert island with Sue Lawley, it would be the natural partner for the King James Bible and the *Complete Works of Shakespeare*. I would especially like to thank the OUP's press offices for the extended loan of a CD-ROM version, which is equally idiosyncratic, equally cherishable and possibly even more useful.

For etymological inquiries, I have also sometimes used Skeat's *Etymological Dictionary* and the *Dictionary of Word Origins* by Linda and Roger Flavell. Other than that, I swear by Partridge's *Dictionary of Slang*, as revised by Paul Beale. Then there's Brewer's *Dictionary of Phrase & Fable*, and an ancient Chambers *Cyclopaedia of English Literature* found in a junk-shop, which seems to include an entry on anyone in English who wrote so much as a postcard.

For comprehensive coverage of the English language I recommend David Crystal's encyclopaedia. I also recommend Bill Bryson's two books on English, *Mother Tongue* and *Made in America*, which pioneered the art of being both informative and funny.

I use numerous foreign language and specialist dictionaries, and have a growing collection of dictionaries of new words, slang, jargon and so on, notably those from Oxford, Bloomsbury, Macmillan and Hodder & Stoughton. I particularly value the works of Jonathon Green and Tony Thorne, who are keeping alive the spirit of the lone word-hunter at a time when many reference books seem to be created by computers at the behest of marketing departments.

That said, this book has benefited enormously from developments in technology. The full-text CDs of various national newspapers in public libraries enabled me to track down current uses of words and phrases. As well as the *OED* CD-ROM, I also use full-text searchable versions of the King James Bible and the *Complete Works of Shakespeare*.

The Internet is now an essential part of the *Frantic Semantics* process. Aside from the general resources of the Net, and searchable texts of numerous great works, there is masses of material about the English language itself. Thanks are due again to the pioneering efforts of Jonathon Green, a.k.a. 'The Word Wizard', and Michael Quinion, both of whom run excellent wide-ranging sites.

I would also like to thank Emma Soames, who introduced 'Frantic Semantics' in the *Telegraph* magazine and hired me to write them, and Rachel Simhon, who was an inspiration as the first person to edit the column. I would also like to thank my wife, Deborah, and my sons, Edward and Frederick, whose way with words defies paraphrase.

Searching for the 'real' meaning of a word may be misguided. But trying to establish what a word means now, and what it has meant in the past, and how it has been used, and by whom, is both a worthwhile thing to do and a great pleasure.

Someone once said that most people think in paragraphs, and clever people think in sentences, but a genius thinks in individual words. It's something we should all try from time to time.

Absolutely

Have you noticed the way 'absolutely' is replacing the word 'yes'? Like this: 'Are you going to the pub?' 'Absolutely!'

It sounds a product of our own, excitable age, but this verbal tic has been with us for most of the century. A simple 'yes' has rarely been enthusiastic enough. Hence 'Yes indeed!' and things worse: 'Certainly', 'Too true' and the creepy 'Surely!'.

Those who use 'absolutely' as an 'intensifier' of this sort are in good company. Said to be American, it is recorded first (1892) in Mark Twain. But it is even found in the penultimate chapter of Joyce's *Ulysses*, in which Leopold Bloom tells his wife Molly about his day's adventures, leaving out the naughty bits.

For those who didn't get that far – it happens – the story is told through question and answer. 'Was the narration otherwise unaltered by modifications?' asks the unnamed catechist. 'Absolutely,' comes the reply.

Interestingly, this 'absolutely' has its own pronunciation, with heavy stress on 'lute'. In its other main use, as an adverb of degree (in 'absolutely fabulous', for instance), the stress falls on 'abs'. That, too, is an intensification. It's an emphatic alternative to 'very'.

But the word, which comes from the Latin *absolutus*, meaning 'free' or 'complete', once had specific meanings: 'separately', 'unconditionally' and 'unrestrictedly'. Monarchs, for instance, could be said to rule 'absolutely'.

But if our current use is sloppy, it is also well established. 'Absolutely' only appeared in English in the fifteenth century and by the end of the sixteenth, people were already being described as 'absolutely skilful' or 'absolutely valorous'. Is that our modern idiom? Absolutely.

For some, however, this intensifier was not intense enough. In our own century we have had 'absoballylutely' and 'absobloodylutely'. Such 'infixes', in which modifying elements are dropped into a word, are rare in English. But perhaps not rare enough.

Actually

Listen to the way small children use the word 'actually'. 'Actually, I'm not hungry,' they say, or 'I'm actually doing painting now.' Or, 'Teddy's a boy, actually.' They seem to sprinkle the word around at random, with no regard for syntax or meaning.

But then so do we: perhaps that's where they got it from. 'Actually' is as ubiquitous in current speech as 'basically' and 'hopefully'. But it has never attracted as much odium as either of those words, despite being at least as meaningless: 'Actually, we're closed'; 'It's *Dr* Jones, actually'; 'It's actually a matter of money'; 'Actually, Jim, if you look at my recent speech . . .'

Was 'actually' always like this? No. It was once quite a serious word. To quote Thomas Hobbes's *Leviathan*, of 1651, 'Christ shall come to judge the world, and actually to governe his owne people.'

'Actually' in this context means 'in person' or 'through his actions'. Or, as we might say today, 'in a hands-on way'. The source of 'actually' was the French *actuel*, coming from the Latin *actus*, an action. *Actuel* was taken into English in the fourteenth century to make the distinction between 'original sin', the sin we inherit, and 'actual sin', the sins we manage to do ourselves.

The French *actuel* also means 'real' and 'at the present time', and 'actually' reflects both meanings. In a phrase such as 'what politicians actually earn', the adverb means 'in practice' as opposed to 'in theory'.

Dictionaries note that 'actually' also means 'as a matter of fact'. This is the tiny sliver of significance that lurks behind our modern, meaningless 'actually'.

This 'actually' is used particularly in asserting some statement that might seem surprising or incredible. You find this most vividly expressed in those car stickers that say, 'Actually, I *do* own the road'.

Adult

Gresham's Law, which states that 'bad money drives out good', is much bandied about by the self-appointed guardians of English. In the case of 'adult', though, they may have a point.

Formerly a straightforward adjective meaning 'full-grown', 'adult' is now a word to use with care. Try, for instance, stepping into the children's department at W. H. Smith and asking if they could direct you to the 'adult games' or the 'adult videos'.

In many contexts – see the Internet for details – the word has become a euphemism for 'salacious' or 'pornographic'. If you want something innocent, but intended for those of mature years, you have to say 'for adults'. The major exception to this rule is 'adult education', which has never been remotely sexy.

This suggestive use of 'adult' is said to be American, but the suspicion is that it started here. 'Unusual adult photo sets' appeared as a 'free exciting offer' in the classifieds of the *New Musical Express* as long ago as 1958. Well, it beat skiffle.

For a while, the word went equipped with nervous inverted commas whenever the sexual implication was intended. But they are going. One American dictionary gives 'full-grown' as its first definition – but 'pornographic' is its second.

Since the seventeenth century, the Latinate 'adult' – from *adolescere*, to grow – has been used alongside the Germanic 'grown' or 'grown-up'. Originally, 'adult' referred to physical maturity. Only in our century has it come to imply mature attitudes or grown-up subject matter. Whether that definition continues to make sense is open to discussion.

'Adultery', by the way, comes from a different Latin root: *adulter-*, identified by some as a combination of *ad-*, meaning 'to', and *alter*, meaning 'another'. An adulterer is someone who turns 'to another'.

So the counselling fraternity are right. Adultery has nothing to do with being 'adult', at least on the level of etymology.

Agenda

These days, everyone has an 'agenda', even those who think that 'minutes' are a unit of time and 'speaking through the chair' is an unusual kind of ventriloquism.

An 'agenda' used to be a list of things to discuss in a formal meeting: either that, or the piece of paper on which such a list was written, properly called the 'agenda paper'. Today, an 'agenda' is a list of grievances, demands or plans close to the heart of a particular group or individual, and rarely open to discussion at all.

There are 'social agendas', 'moral agendas', 'political agendas' and, in relationships, 'emotional agendas'. There are also 'hidden agendas', which is where you say one thing and mean another, without necessarily being a politician.

Technically, 'agenda' is plural, like 'data' and 'media', although that seems to have escaped the nation's pedants. It is the plural of the Latin *agendum*, meaning 'that which is to be done'. This makes it part of a family with *memorandum* ('that which is to be remembered') and *curriculum vitae*, ('that which is to be invented'). Offices are a bastion of classicism, possibly because they are the last places in which people can get away with acting like Caligula.

The *agenda* (sometimes Anglicized to the 'agends') were originally the practical demands of a Christian life, as opposed to the *credenda*, the beliefs. By the eighteenth century, 'agenda' had come to mean both the normal church service and a notebook containing a list of things to do.

Modern office usage is nineteenth century, but the word is often used figuratively, as in 'What's on the agenda for tonight?' The political twist seems to have come from America, where every minority has its own 'agenda'. Sadly, as any efficient secretary will tell you, more than one agenda at a time is a recipe for chaos.

Aggressive

When did being 'aggressive' become a good thing? Job advertisements show employers desperate to find 'aggressive' staff and 'aggressive' managers to pursue 'aggressive' approaches and practise 'aggressive' strategies.

True, it's a dog-eat-dog world. But how are matters improved if the people who run supermarkets are, to quote one dictionary, 'disposed to attack others'? You don't want that quality in your generals, let alone those who are flogging you baked beans.

'Aggressive' is a nineteenth-century adjective from 'aggression', a military term first found in the seventeenth century and meaning 'an unprovoked attack'. Both come from the medieval Latin verb *aggressare*, meaning to launch such an action. 'Aggression' and 'aggressive' have invariably referred to the practice of picking a fight, whether in the playground or as a global strategy.

So who made aggression into a good thing? The finger points at psychoanalysis. Sigmund Freud (and his early English translators) always used the word disparagingly. But, in 1908, unhappy with Freud's emphasis on sex, his disciple Alfred Adler developed the idea of *Aggressionstrieb*, the 'aggression drive'. He meant self-assertion and the desire to achieve.

Adler's own *Aggressionstrieb* was such that he marched straight out of the Freudian movement. But like his other ideas, the 'inferiority complex' and 'life-style', Adler's benevolent 'aggression' was soon picked up and used by people who had never heard of him.

What remains obscure, however, is why it became a key term among the no-nonsense retailing folk of Canada. It was there that our precise modern usage first surfaced, as a synonym for 'enterprising' or 'energetic'. In 1930, an advertisement in a Vancouver newspaper asked for an 'aggressive clothing salesman'. In 1956, a similar ad in Winnipeg suggested that 'only aggressive men need apply'.

This secured Canada's place in the history of English usage. But there may have been better places to buy your socks.

Ambient

Success in the music world is transient. One minute you are the word on the street, the next you are forgotten. Such has been the fate of 'ambient'.

In the mid-1990s, 'ambient' shot to fame as a label for a kind of etiolated disco music, *sans* tune, *sans* rhythm, *sans* everything. Now it has had to revert to its previous life as a workaday adjective.

From the Latin *ambire*, meaning 'to encircle', it first appeared in English at the end of the sixteenth century. Francis Bacon was an early enthusiast. In 1605, taking a break from writing Shakespeare's plays, he wrote that 'Consumption is caused by depredation of innate spirit, and depredation of ambient aire.' Quite wrong, but the word, meaning 'surrounding', has proved more durable than his medical insights.

Thereafter the word prospered in both poetry and science. Milton wrote of 'ambient light'. Pope described 'ambient clouds'. And E. A. Wilcox, in his seminal work *Electric Heating* (1928), introduced the idea of 'ambient temperatures'.

Later came 'ambient noise', noise no one really notices, followed by 'ambient music', music no one really notices. This is not a new idea. Early in the century, Erik Satie experimented with compositions designed to be ignored, but fell into despair when people insisted on listening to them. No such danger with the modern version, which started with Brian Eno's 1978 *Music for Airports*, catalogue number Ambient #1.

'Ambient' was the authentic soundtrack of the Major era, which perhaps explains why it was so unmemorable. But what better accompaniment for an 'ambient meal'? This is food trade jargon for something that lurks in your cupboard at room temperature until you warm it up.

The first was the Vesta curry of 1962, but these days there is a huge range. 'Ambient' music may have gone, but the Pot Noodle marches on.

Anomaly

Anomaly

'We have had an anomaly.' That remarkable understatement, as $55 million worth of rocket and military satellite exploded in front of her, thirteen seconds after taking off from Cape Canaveral, showed that launch commentator Anne Toulouse had the Right Stuff.

To the rest of us, an 'anomaly' is a discrepancy in our expenses, not what the newspapers described as a 'cascade of flaming debris'. But understatement is a tradition in the world of rocketry and space exploration.

When Apollo 13 went badly wrong, it was, 'Houston, we have a problem.' Then there was the explosion that destroyed the Challenger space shuttle and its crew, briefly described as a 'malfunction'.

The instinct is to underplay. As Tom Wolfe pointed out in *The Right Stuff*, the language of space is unflappable, like that of the early test pilots. And then there's military tradition, in which a man is only allowed to curse if he has had his leg blown off – and then nothing stronger than 'Damn!'

But why 'anomaly'? Its origin is the Greek noun *anomalia*, meaning 'irregularity' or 'unevenness'. First recorded in English in the sixteenth century, 'anomaly' was used for physical irregularities, for instance in the movements of astronomical bodies. Later it came to mean deviations from the social or natural order.

For a while, there was a word 'anomal', meaning 'an odd thing' as opposed to the 'quality of oddness'. You don't have to be David Attenborough, however, to see the difficulties involved in talking about 'anomals among the animals'. So 'anomaly' came to do both jobs.

Recently, 'anomaly' has become a favourite of the computer industry. They use it when they know something has gone wrong, but they daren't say precisely what or why. It points no fingers and, more importantly, accepts no blame.

You can see how, as an employee of the rocket launcher company, Ms Toulouse might have arrived at this particular word.

Anorak

Apparently an 'anorak' used to be something you wore. These days, it's something you are.

In the same way that a 'suit' has come to mean a representative of corporate orthodoxy, an 'anorak' is someone earnest, obsessive and lacking in social graces.

'Anoraks' are usually said to be obsessed with railway engines ('train-spotter' is almost a synonym) or science fiction or computers or hi-fi (in which case try 'propeller-head'). But just about any overwhelming, and overwhelmingly male, obsession will do.

There's even an adjective. Radio One's decline, for instance, has been attributed to its becoming 'too anorak for its own good'.

'Anorak' is a Greenland Eskimo word for a weatherproof jacket of skin or cloth, with – and here we get to the nub – a hood attached. It came into English in the 1920s and 1930s in descriptions of the traditional costume of the Eskimo woman.

By 1950, similar garments had been adopted by (male) moun-taineers. Then, in 1959, its transition into civilian life seemed complete, *Vogue* featured a 'poplin anorak with attached hood'. Anoraks have rarely appeared in *Vogue* since, though they are very important in caravanning.

But what of the new sense? It is said to have developed on British campuses in the mid-1980s as a term of abuse for those misguided students who insisted on jeopardizing their own popularity by working. Grinding through demanding science courses, they rarely had time to develop the fashionable dress sense or dazzling social skills of their tormentors.

Today's world, though, is a technological place. Those who sat at the front and asked questions are destined to triumph over those who sat at the back and looked cool: think of Bill Gates, the richest man in the world. The revenge of the anoraks is upon us.

Anthem

Have you been in a record shop lately and noticed all those compilation albums: *Club Anthems*, *Hip-Hop Anthems*, not to mention *Anthems*?

And that's only the start. Elsewhere you'll find 'national anthems' – try the easy listening section, under military bands – and a whole range of choral and instrumental compositions with a similar designation.

What a versatile musical form, you might think, encompassing everything from trip-hop to George Frideric Handel. But few of these 'anthems' are the real thing. Even the 'National Anthem' is a fraud. 'Anthem' came from the Greek *antiphona*, meaning something like 'sounds replying'. The medieval Church used the term to describe music in which two voices or choirs sing in turn. Mispronounced by generations of Englishmen, the word evolved into 'anthem'.

'Anthems' were supposed to be based on religious prose. Songs based on poetry were called hymns. The 'National Anthem', for instance, is technically a hymn. It is also the only tune ever incorporated into a musical bustle that played when its owner – Queen Victoria – sat down. But that's another story.

The word 'anthem' was subsequently applied to the national 'hymns' of other countries and, more recently, to other songs for mass singing, notably the 'terrace anthems' of football fans. 'You'll Never Walk Alone' is an example. 'You're Going Home By ****ing Ambulance', on the other hand, is more of a chant.

When rock music moved into the football stadiums, bands struggled to write songs with singalong appeal. These epics ('We Are the Champions', 'Sailing' etc.) were duly described as 'anthems' by teenage scribblers tired of the word 'song'. The same ennui may explain the record companies' current enthusiasm for the word.

Could you sing along to any of the numbers featured on such compilations as *Club Anthems*? Who knows? No one would be able to hear you.

Architecture

At the height of the Bosnian War, the BBC reported that the British Defence Secretary had made a speech about 'the new security architecture of Europe'. What did he mean? Doric columns on all new aircraft hangars? Or a wall around the Balkans?

Neither, in fact. In referring to 'architecture', Michael Portillo was merely using a vogue word for anything complicated, from the organization of large machines to the defence of nations.

We are right, however, to associate the word with bricks and mortar. It made its English debut in Tudor times, in the title of a book about the monuments of Greece and Italy. 'Architect' arrived at the same time, an adaptation of the Greek *architekton*, meaning 'master builder'.

Today, 'architect' is a legally protected title: 'architects' require years of training and a thick skin. But 'architect' and 'architecture' have always been used figuratively as well. In *Tamburlaine the Great*, written around 1590, Christopher Marlowe talks about 'the wondrous architecture of the world'. The Great Architect, as you know, is God.

In our own century, 'architecture' has been used of musical compositions, of bodily organs, molecules and even the odd virus. But in more respectful times, all 'architecture' implied a single 'architect'. That is no longer the case.

'Architecture' is, for instance, a common term in computing, where things are built by teams of cola-guzzling youths rather than by individual creators. An IBM document of 1964 defined 'architecture' as 'the conceptual structure and functional behaviour' of a computer, as opposed to its layout: its mind, not its brain.

And 'security architecture', as borrowed by the former Defence Secretary, is itself a computer term. It means the way computer systems are arranged to exclude viruses, hackers and other malevolent elements. You can see that this might be a seductive analogy for contemporary Europe.

Atrium

The 'atrium' is one of the joys of city life: a glazed entrance hall
where you wait while a woman with a computer tells you she has no
record of your appointment. It should not be confused with the
'galleria': a glazed shopping mall where you wait while a woman with
a till tells you she has no stamps, tea bags or string, but that she does
have some very nice healing crystals from Brazil.

The alacrity with which these terms from architectural history
have been embraced and subverted speaks volumes for the philistin-
ism of our age. The 'atrium' in a Roman house was a main room
open to the sky, with a central basin for the collection of rainwater.
Modern 'atriums' (*atria* tend to be the chambers of the heart) have
roofs, not that they can dispense with the water basin.

By the time of Cicero, *c*.50 BC, the *Atrium libertatis* (or 'hall of
liberty') was the building in Rome where slaves were subjected to
various humiliations and tortures: no wonder the word rang a bell
with the developers of contemporary office accommodation.

A 'galleria', on the other hand, was a formal room in an Italian
Renaissance palace, often decorated with frescos and sculptures of
real quality. Later it came to mean a charming arcade of individual
shops. Now it's another word for Arndale Centre.

From the sixteenth to the nineteenth centuries, 'atrium' and
'galleria' were used in English writing about ancient buildings. Then,
in the early 1960s, American architects and critics ransacked the
dictionary for new terms with which to elucidate the splendours of a
series of impressively tawdry hotels and lucratively twee shopping
centres. 'Atrium' and 'galleria' worked a treat.

Recently, we have made the words our own: the *architectural*
vocabulary, however, is a less successful import. Have you been to
Canary Wharf?

Attitude

When you hear that someone's got 'attitude', what sort of 'attitude' do you expect? Helpful, co-operative, pleasant? Of course not. These days, any 'attitude' is a bad 'attitude'.

This is a comparatively recent development. As late as 1984, dictionaries defined 'attitude' as a person's posture towards society, with no mention of whether that was generally favourable or not.

By the early 1990s, however, that was changing. To say 'he's got attitude', no indefinite article being necessary, was to say that someone was sullen and full of hostility, especially for authority. The new usage was said to be Black American, a scornful adaptation of such expressions as 'negative attitude' and 'attitude problem', pinned on them by those in authority.

Such an outlook is almost invariably apparent in a person's physical stance: and that is what 'attitude' really means. It is a French word, derived from the Latin *aptitudinem*, meaning suitability or fitness for a task (which also gave us 'aptitude').

It came into English in the seventeenth century through the fine arts. 'Attitude' was the posture of a figure in a sculpture or painting. Later it came to mean a posture that implied a mental state: you could, for instance, adopt a 'pious attitude' or a 'subservient attitude'. Only in the nineteenth century did it become possible to talk about an 'attitude of mind', meaning a predominant disposition, whether habitual or deliberately adopted.

'Attitude' is also used in dancing, to mean the way you hold yourself. But it has a more technical sense as well. An 'attitude' is a particular form of arabesque, apparently modelled on Giovanni Bologna's statue of Mercury, in which the dancer stands on one leg with the other extended behind.

This is probably not where our contemporary 'attitude' came from.

Audit

Have you been lucky enough to experience an 'audit'?

Until recently, the only people who encountered the word were bookkeepers and accountants. Once a year, the auditors would look at a firm's books and declare they were accurate and honest. Or they would not, in which case another firm of auditors would be found.

Nowadays, the word 'audit' is used for all manner of investigations, inquiries and checks. Can staff do their jobs? Have a 'skills audit'. Are the office computers full of games and rude e-mails? Time for a 'technology audit'. Where does all the photocopier paper go? Hold an 'eco-audit'.

And it's not just about office life. The nation's hospitals have 'clinical audits' to see how many they cure and how many they, er, don't. Your local pest-control man can even offer you an 'infestation audit'.

We probably owe all this to the rise of the accountants. As they grew more influential, during the 1980s, so did their language and methods. Modern managers have learned to start measuring and counting things. Using the word 'audit' suggests the application of cool, mathematical logic to what are really intangible human problems.

If the word has a sinister ring, that may be because 'auditing' is the Scientologists' version of psychotherapy, in which the skills of the therapist, or 'auditor', are complemented by the 'E-meter'. This detects unconscious ailments that can only be removed by further 'auditing'.

This reminds us that 'audit' has its roots in the Latin *audire*, to hear. When the word first appeared in English, in the fifteenth century, the examination and settling of accounts always required an oral hearing.

In subsequent centuries, it was not uncommon for those of a poetic inclination to write of 'the final Audit', by which was meant the Day of Judgement. Compared to which, your forthcoming 'performance audit' will be a piece of cake.

Babe

The recently revived 'babe' is an old word, at least as old as 'baby'. This may come as a shock to the readers of *Loaded*, who probably think they invented it.

'Babe' is thought to have come from the thirteenth-century 'baban' or 'babbon', supposedly imitations of an infant's first sounds. It was the standard form as late as the 1611 King James Bible, after which it was increasingly replaced by its own diminutive, 'baby'.

Its reappearance has several sources, most of them American. Since the nineteenth century, 'baby' has been applied to young women, with varying degrees of respect. The expression 'She's some babe', moreover, was recorded as early as 1915.

Barry White's 'Can't Get Enough Of Your Love, Babe' of 1974 may have something to do with the spread of 'Babe' as a term of address for either sex in Britain during the late 1970s. Then 'Babes', an even less respectable variant, was carried to stardom by Alison Steadman, who built her character around it in Mike Leigh's *Life Is Sweet*.

The current vogue for 'babe' stems from films such as *Bill & Ted's Excellent Adventure* (1988) which spread the argot of Californian youth around the world. The film was a satirical account of a pair of adolescent sexual inadequates, but no one noticed that in the rush to start imitating the way they spoke.

Their lascivious 'babe' spawned numerous variants, including 'book babes', who liked reading, 'Bach babes', who appeared scantily clad on the covers of their own classical records, and 'virtual babes', the absurdly proportioned heroines of computer games. There were also 'Asian babes', a concept enthusiastically embraced by a former editor of the *Sunday Times*.

Oddly, while traditional feminists loathe 'babe' for its 'infantilizing' quality, more recent female cultural commentators have found a better way of expressing their emotional maturity and sexual confidence. They've started applying it to men.

Ballistic

Every day now, someone, somewhere is 'going ballistic'. We know what the phrase means – becoming uncontrollably angry – but quite *why* is another matter.

'Ballistic' actually means 'pertaining to the throwing of missiles', and comes from the Latin *ballista*, itself derived from the Greek for 'to throw'. A ballista, as military historians and those who collected toy soldiers may recall, was a Roman engine of war. A giant crossbow, it was used for firing pointed objects at enemy fortifications.

'Ballista' first appeared here in 1598, when someone was translating Tacitus and, not surprisingly, couldn't think of an English equivalent. The adjective arrived a couple of centuries later in military and scientific uses, notably the 'ballistic pendulum' and the 'ballistic galvanometer'.

The noun 'ballistics' sometimes crops up in television crime series, where it means the police department which investigates the provenance of bullets, another well-known projectile. And then there is 'ballistic missile', a 1950s expression for a rocket which is guided going up, but finds its own way down.

The use of 'ballistic' as a slang expression for 'furious' seems to have arisen spontaneously in the 1980s in America. Both an angry person and a falling missile are 'out of control': perhaps that's the analogy. 'Flying off the handle' is an earlier equivalent, although here the comparison is with the head of a hammer breaking free and hurtling lethally through the air.

In 1988, the expression received approval at the highest level, when President George Bush, defending himself against accusations of being a wimp, declared, 'I get furious. I go ballistic!' Impressed, the nation elected Bill Clinton.

Our own politicians have been accused of 'going ballistic' too, starting with Mrs Thatcher. When applied to her successor, however, the term tended to be used ironically. When John Major went 'ballistic' during Prime Minister's Questions, reported the *Guardian*, 'his voice went from a pipe to a squeak'. Unkind, but not inaccurate.

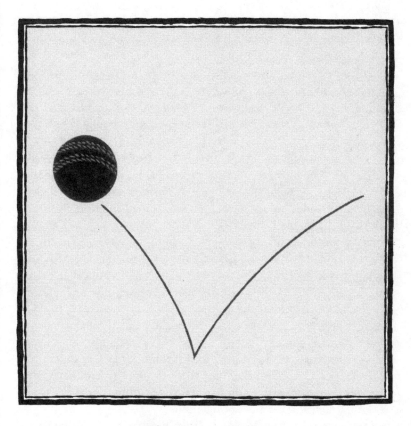

Beauty

Beauty

'Beauty is truth, truth beauty,' wrote John Keats. But he'd never been to a 'beauty department' or spoken to a 'beauty therapist', or he might have changed his mind.

There he would discover that the principal subject of poets and philosophers throughout the centuries has been reduced to a mere commodity. It would seem safe to blame the Americans for this. After all, they started the new century by inventing the 'beauty contest', 'beauty culture' and the 'beauty parlor'.

But that would be unjust. In 1709, the original London *Tatler* mentioned 'The only true Cosmetick or Beauty-Wash in the World'. 'Beauty sleep' appears in a Charles Kingsley novel of 1857, with 'beauty shop' and 'beauty show' following close behind.

Until the eighteenth century, though, 'beauty' had been the real thing, a word signifying perfection, both in appearance and an inherent quality. It arrived here from French in the late thirteenth century, spelt 'bealte' or even 'buute'. The word's origins are in the Late Latin *bellitatem*, the noun from *bellus*, beautiful.

From the late fifteenth century, an attractive woman could be called 'a beauty', an idiom later adapted, particularly in Australia, to mean an exceptionally good example of something. The *OED*'s earliest example is 'Spofforth was bowled by a "beauty" from Mycroft', in an account of an 1882 Australian cricket tour of England. Sometimes this was shortened to 'beaut'. 'Beauty!' is also an Australian expression of approbation.

In the late 1970s, particle physicists discovered two new types of 'quark', the sub-atomic particle. Initially dubbed 'truth' and 'beauty', these were renamed 'top' and 'bottom' after hard-faced physicists complained that the original names were whimsical, though not before the *Daily Telegraph* had pronounced on the subject. '"Beauty" lasts about one tenth of a millionth of a millionth of a second before decaying,' it said, although Keats would have disagreed.

Benchmarking

A group of building society managers on a train are having a lively discussion about their staff. 'Yes,' says one, with a pained expression. 'But have yours been through benchmarking yet?'

It would be nice to think of 'benchmarking' as a charming extra-curricular pursuit for stressed office workers, perhaps involving the carving of inscriptions on park furniture. Sadly, 'benchmarking' is another management tool designed to measure the performance of people as if they were office equipment.

That's not the word's original meaning. A 'bench mark' is a nineteenth-century device, carved by surveyors on walls and rocks as a height reference. You find them on mountains: a horizontal slot with an arrowhead meeting it from beneath.

A bar is inserted into the point where arrow and line meet, and this becomes the 'bench' upon which the levelling is based. A 'bench', as you know, is a long flat seat, and has been since *Beowulf*, c. AD 800.

'Benchmark' has long been used for any fixed point of reference, concrete or abstract: an 1884 book, for instance, talks about stars being the 'bench-marks' of the universe. Nowadays, it has come to mean a standard of excellence, particularly in business and in sport. 'The privatized rail companies have set a new benchmark for customer service,' you might say, if you'd taken leave of your senses.

But the 'benchmarking' of people has another source. Computers are 'benchmarked' by setting them various standard tasks and measuring how long they take. In the case of human beings, the 'benchmark' is the performance of other people doing similar work in other departments or other companies.

Is 'benchmarking' a good thing? Hard to say, but based on what the building society managers had to report, it doesn't seem to be a very popular one.

Blag

A local paper reporter of my acquaintance once rang the police station and asked, 'What's the SP on the sparklers blag?' – only to rephrase the question when it became clear that the policeman at the other end didn't have a clue what he meant.

The suspicion was that the reporter had picked up this embarrassing argot from television rather than the mean streets of south London. 'SP' meant 'starting price', hence 'latest news'; 'sparklers' meant jewellery; and 'blag' meant a robbery. That, at least, was the real thing.

To 'blag' has meant to rob, usually with violence, since the latter part of the last century. Originally, it meant a simple bag-snatching. But by the 1930s, a 'blag' was a wages snatch or a bank job, those staples of mid-1970s television.

These days, however, to 'blag' something is not so much to steal it as to scrounge it, or con it out of someone. You might, for instance, 'blag' your way into a show, or 'blag' something valuable on the grounds that you were 'evaluating' it.

This 'blag' has some similarities with the French *blague*, meaning a joke or a hoax: you 'blag' by pretending to be something you are not. More likely, though, it is an adaptation of the criminal 'blag'.

Some have derived 'blag' from a Yorkshire dialect word for gathering blackberries, but it probably comes from 'blackguard'. In the sixteenth century, the lowest ranking kitchen servants were called the 'black guard' because they spent their time with filthy pots and pans.

By the nineteenth century, a 'blackguard', pronounced 'blaggard', was a street urchin, a person of low character or a villain. As that word has faded away, so 'blagger' and 'blag' have risen to prominence, the latter making its debut in an 1885 account of a street crime. There would seem to be a connection.

Bless!

The cooing monosyllable 'Bless!' seems to be exclusively female. Uttered in response to some loveable gesture or foible on the part of man, child or animal, it is a colloquial shortening of 'Ah, bless him!'

Obviously, 'Bless him!' is itself a cut-down, secularized form of the earlier 'God bless him.' To 'bless' someone is to wish them well, or, more precisely, to ask God to show them His favour.

The verb 'to bless' is rather odd. It appeared, as *bloedsian*, before the last millennium, formed from a Teutonic word meaning 'blood'. In heathen religions this had made perfect sense: things devoted to the gods, or favoured by them, were daubed in blood.

When Christianity arrived in Britain, a word was required to describe the bestowing of God's favour on someone. The Latin word was *benedicere*, meaning 'to speak well of', but the missionaries used *bloedsian*, possibly because of the way it connected pre-Christian rituals with the animal sacrifices featured in the pre-vegetarian Old Testament. Thereafter priests themselves could 'bless' someone or something by saying appropriate words or making the sign of the cross. Those who were on their own and afraid could cross themselves.

People say, 'Bless you!' ('God bless you!' until quite recently) when someone sneezes. This may stem from the belief that we are susceptible to evil spirits when we sneeze. Or it may reflect the belief, not so far-fetched in ancient times, that a sneeze is a precursor of death. At that point you would need to be on good terms with God.

The custom is sometimes said to have been started by St Gregory, but he was probably too busy, what with arranging the conversion of England and introducing Gregorian chant, thereby ensuring that fourteen centuries later the album charts are full of adorable singing monks. Bless!

Bonding

Bonding

The abuse heaped upon the Conservative Party when it started holding annual seaside 'bonding' sessions has made this a difficult word to use with a straight face. This is bad news for the management gurus and motivational witch doctors who favour it.

The Tories' 'bonding' is a variant on 'male bonding', a term used with various degrees of derision in reference to such masculine pursuits as rugby, rock-climbing and sitting in the pub. There is no such thing as 'female bonding', of course, intimacy between women being standard practice rather than an aberration worthy of scientific study.

'Male bonding' is always linked to the American 'men's movement', which encourages men to gather in remote places, banging drums and weeping, a spectacle strangely reminiscent of the Tories' seaside gatherings. 'Bonding', in the sense of a psychological relationship, is prominent in American dictionaries, but absent from ours.

In origin, 'bonding' is a seventeenth-century term for methods of joining bricks and pieces of wood: a 'bond' was originally the rope or strap used to shackle a prisoner. The physicists of the nineteenth century borrowed 'bonding' as a term for the way atoms are connected, not least so that they could write about something they could neither explain nor picture.

From physics, the term spread into zoology, where 'bonding' described the social and sexual behaviour of animals. Humans came next, starting with primitive peoples, who had 'bonding' where we have 'committed relationships'.

In 1976, American paediatricians Marshall Klaus and John Kennell used the term to describe what happens between mothers and newborn babies in their book *Maternal Infant Bonding*. This dominated neo-natal practice until 1993, when another book suggested 'bonding' was 'a scientific fiction'.

That has not, however, prevented its continued use as a panacea for failing sports teams, factious companies and unloved political parties.

Brand

Do you remember that ancient cinema commercial, advertising the peculiar hamburgers they used to sell in the foyer? 'Get 'em where you see this brand!' shouts a cowboy. And with that, a big 'W' is sizzled on to the side of a cartoon buffalo.

That tells you just about everything you need to know about a word that is currently mesmerizing British business. Every day, people in suits are 'managing the brand', 'building the brand', and 'growing the brand', though rarely does anyone talk about welding it on to the hide of a passing herbivore.

By 'brands' they mean the names of their products, which they are pledged to defend with their lives, at least until they throw them away and use something that sounds better in German.

The hamburger advert had it right. A 'brand' was originally something you burned on to an object to demonstrate your ownership. It is Old English for 'something burning' or 'something burnt', and hence for the mark made by a burning iron, whether on animal hide or human skin.

In Britain, convicted felons were marked on the cheek with an 'F', as late as 1822. The word was adopted in a commercial sense only five years after that: someone had 'branded' his name on his boxes.

Later the word 'brand' began to apply not to the mark but to the goods themselves, so that by the end of the nineteenth century people were able to ask for their 'usual brand' of snuff or hair oil.

The word's current vogue may stem from David Ogilvy, the advertising man of the 1950s, who said that 'every advertisement should be thought of as a contribution to the brand image. It follows that your advertising should consistently project the same image, year after year.'

That's one lesson the hamburger people never forgot.

Brilliant

A telephone conversation: 'Is Susie there?' 'Not until Friday.' 'Brilliant.'

What's so 'brilliant' about that? Dictionaries suggest that the word is slang for 'excellent'. But there's nothing 'excellent' about the person you want not being there. Instead, 'brilliant' stands in for a whole sentence: 'It was excellent of you to tell me that: thank you.' 'Brilliant' is quicker, but 'OK', 'All right' or 'Ta' would have done just as well.

It's the kind of conversation that you hear all the time, and demonstrates the descent of 'brilliant' into near-meaninglessness, as little more than an emphatic expression of assent. It wasn't always like that.

'Brilliant' arrived late in the seventeenth century, a simple Anglicization of the French *brillant*, shining. It has always applied to light and glittering things. The noun 'brilliant' is a particular type of diamond. It's also, it is said, gay slang for a particularly flamboyant homosexual.

In the eighteenth century, 'brilliant' began to be used figuratively, to describe actions or qualities that were particularly striking. A century later, it began to be applied to exceptionally clever people, and it still is, but with a reassuring implication that there is something flashy and trivial about them.

The use of the adjective to mean 'excellent' is reckoned to be new. Most trace its arrival to the late 1970s or early 1980s, although there is good evidence of it being used in precisely this sense in South Africa as early as 1971, among surfers.

When it arrived here, it was in the language of teenagers. 'Brilliant' was followed by 'Brill!', which subsequently disappeared, although not before making its mark on literature. 'Maybe he's brill in the bag,' a character muses in Martin Amis's 1983 novel *Money*, a 'brilliant' book in most senses of the word.

Buddy

On the wall in the municipal swimming baths is the following poster: 'Come Swimming – And Bring Your Buddy.'

So what have we here? A simple two-for-one special offer? Or – and it helps to know that this is a caring borough – a special session for those with AIDS and their volunteer helpers?

As it happens, it was the former. But it just goes to show the confusion that can arise when society finds a new use for a word without erasing the old one.

The AIDS 'buddy' arrived in the early 1980s in New York. Those in the later stages of the disease were provided with an unpaid assistant to give them both material and emotional support.

This was a new application for the 'buddy system', an arrangement first used in the military and amongst participants in dangerous sports. But it is also used by American schoolchildren, who are encouraged to 'buddy up' before they do anything frightening: switching off the television, for instance, or taking a walk.

But what of 'buddy' itself? It is American, as you expected, and means 'friend' or 'comrade', although it is also a word this democratic nation uses to express outright hostility. It first appeared in print in America in the 1850s, said to be a baby-talk approximation of 'brother'.

Alternatively, 'buddy' might derive from the British 'butty'. Not the sliced-bread sandwich, but either a Cheshire/Lancashire dialect term for 'mate' or a Welsh or gypsy diminutive of 'brother'.

Recent years have seen the arrival of the 'buddy movie', in which two big stars snarl at each other for twenty minutes before reluctantly teaming up to triumph over the audience's indifference. *Butch Cassidy and the Sundance Kid* was the first – and the last good one.

To separate him from such trivia, the AIDS volunteer is now sometimes awarded a capital 'b'.

Bung

The nation owes Alan Sugar, boss of Amstrad and Tottenham Hotspur, a debt. Not for creating the word processor everyone could afford – and no one could work – but for introducing us to the word 'bung'.

Sugar was wrangling with Terry Venables, his former partner at Spurs, in the High Court, scene of the only real action in British football. Sugar quoted Venables as saying that one famous manager 'liked a bung'.

He wasn't suggesting that the man took a scholarly interest in corks, plugs and stoppers. He meant he favoured a personal cash inducement to expedite a transfer.

This 'bung' was first used by the police and criminals, two professions divided by a common language. To give a policeman a 'bung' is to pay him a substantial bribe. A small bribe has its own name – 'a drink'.

Reassuringly, none of this is new. The expression dates from the 1930s. More recently, according to *Muvver Tongue*, a 1980 study of Cockney, 'bung' has been used in that community – of which Venables and Sugar are elders – as a word for any sort of bribery.

Recent newspapers show everyone taking a 'bung': footballers, football managers, politicians, lawyers, businessmen, and the entire electorate.

The etymology is interesting. The stopper came first, in the fifteenth century, probably adapted from the Middle Dutch *bonghe*. There was also a verb 'to bung', meaning 'to stop up'.

In the nineteenth century, a slang verb 'to bung', meaning 'to throw', appeared from nowhere. It is from this, presumably, that the current 'bung' derives: 'Bung him a few quid and you won't have any trouble.'

But here's a twist. Between the sixteenth and eighteenth centuries, a 'bung' was what pickpockets and cutpurses called the bag of money they made off with. A coincidence, probably, but rather an instructive one.

Butt

Given our love of Americanisms, it's not surprising to stumble upon, for instance, a 'Butt & Thigh Workout' on British breakfast television.

Even so, it is rare to hear Britons use the word 'butt', except in reference to barrels filled with rainwater and the ends of cigarettes.

In the US, 'butt' almost always means the buttocks, although it is amusing to see that the *New American Webster Handy College Dictionary* omits that definition, presumably for prudish reasons.

It suggests that 'butt' means a wine cask, the thick end of something, or the target of a joke. Presumably it also thinks, as is technically true, that 'butt-head' means one end of a plank.

There have been, at various times, fourteen different 'butts', including a flatfish, the raised areas of a ploughed field and a two-wheeled cart used in Cornwall. Only one has a backside connection.

In Britain, we use the plural of the word 'buttock' when we are talking about the human rump. 'Buttock' is said to be a diminutive formed from 'butt', in the same way that hillock was formed from hill. The only snag is that 'buttock' came first, in the thirteenth century.

The rear end 'butt' is first recorded in *c.*1450, as the English word for the Latin *lumbus*, the loins. But we have rarely used it for the human posterior. It has been used figuratively, for the blunt end of things, and for the rumps of various farm animals.

It acquired its American nuance in the Wild West, where, as early as 1860, such phrases as 'I fell on my butt' and 'he kicked my butt' were heard for the first time.

This seems a slightly mysterious development, until you remember that out there cattle – and the words used to describe them – were much more important than people.

Buzz

You may have read about young women who put cameras in their bedrooms and broadcast the pictures over the Internet. A harmless pursuit, said one psychologist. At least for the women.

The danger, he told one newspaper, was to the viewers. 'If people get buzzed up and rewarded from watching there is a potential for addiction.'

This 'buzzed up', meaning stimulated, is new. But 'buzz' itself has been with us for a while. Often used to denote a drug-induced mood change, it can also mean a 'high' produced by some legal activity. 'I admit, it gives me a buzz,' said one man in a much-repeated television advert. He was talking about working in a bank.

'Buzz' is not a product of the 'E' era. It was heard first in America in the 1940s, identified as 'a kick', 'a thrill', or, unambiguously, 'the influence of a drug'.

From the 1960s onwards, drug terminology spread widely. Here's *The Times* in 1983, striking a familiar note: 'Some players get a "buzz" from the game [of Space Invaders] and that might explain why they become addicted.'

Whereas the nineteenth-century 'kick' seems to make an analogy with a blow from a donkey's hoof, or perhaps the recoil of a gun, 'buzz' seems to refer to an electric shock.

But the word 'buzz' implied excitement long before either recreational drugs or electricity. Originally, it represented the sound of bees. But by the Restoration it meant the hubbub of a busy room or a fashionable subject for conversation. In 1678, the critic Thomas Rymer wrote, in a study of classical poetry, 'All the buzz in Athens was now about virtue.'

He could have been writing last week, except for the bit about virtue.

Caring

The words 'care' and 'caring', once used about the nobler instincts of humanity, are on the way to disrepute, and politicians are to blame. They bolted together two favourite words to create 'care in the community', a policy that proved to have little to do with either.

'Care' itself is an old word, derived from the Old English *caru*, meaning trouble or sorrow. The verb meant 'to grieve', then 'to be concerned about', and most recently 'to have a fondness for'.

Following a 1932 law dealing with 'Juveniles in need of Care and Protection', all sorts of 'care'-mongering began, giving us 'in care' and the 'care order'. 'Care' now acquired a suggestion of 'control'.

The adjective 'caring' is first recorded in 1966, in the context of 'caring television': later it was appropriated, in conjunction with 'sharing', by the Co-op chain.

The expression 'caring profession', meanwhile, dates from the mid-1970s, when it was applied to social workers. Unfortunately, this was followed by a series of incidents in which members of the 'caring profession' appeared not to have given a damn.

Since then the 'caring professions' have grown to include doctors, nurses, dentists, psychiatrists, teachers, childminders, counsellors and many more. When the 'caring professionals' clock off, however, things are left to the 'carers', heroic figures whose personal responsibility it is to look after someone sick, aged or disabled. Unlike members of the 'caring professions', 'carers' tend not to be paid.

A 1990 law introduced the expression 'community care' for its rules about long-term provision for the elderly. This was quite distinct from 'care in the community', the policy of closing psychiatric hospitals and letting the disturbed fend for themselves, helped, if at all, by their 'carers'.

In such a 'caring' world, it is no wonder that it is common to hear people saying to one another, by way of valediction, 'Take care.'

Challenged

The vogue for the word 'challenged' as a kindly euphemism for 'handicapped' was short-lived, at least on this side of the Atlantic.

No sooner had this well-meaning innovation arrived than it disappeared under a welter of jokes. Someone fat would be described as 'gravitationally challenged'. Someone short was 'vertically challenged'. Someone ugly was 'aesthetically challenged'. Few of us have ever heard the expression used sincerely, but we all know the jokes.

So who did use it, if anyone? Suspicion falls on the Americans, world leaders in the manufacture of euphemisms. The first recorded use was in the *New York Times* of April 1985, where disabled skiers were called 'physically challenged'. In 1987, the *Los Angeles Times* countered with 'mentally challenged' and thereafter the floodgates were opened.

If anyone here used the expression without irony, it has gone unrecorded. Mostly we used it to make fun of our over-sensitive American cousins.

But why 'challenged'? Historically, to 'challenge' is to confront: 'Who goes there, friend or foe?' It comes from the Late Latin *calumniare*, to accuse falsely. A challenge was a serious matter, usually ending in a fight.

In our own namby-pamby era, however, the 'challenges' are less obvious. You can be 'challenged' by some sort of handicap, as in the American euphemisms. Or the 'challenge' can be an irksome task, such as worming the cat.

But in the language of marketing, 'challenging' is increasingly used for things that barely excite our curiosity: a film, a book or a new brand of soap.

Meanwhile, self-help gurus, therapists and management theorists preaching positive thinking require their disciples to speak of 'challenges' rather than 'problems'. You are supposed to announce, 'I'm sorry I'm late. I had a bit of a challenge when my train was cancelled.'

As with the euphemisms, however, the 'challenge' for most British people will be to keep from laughing.

Cherished

Have you ever fancied fitting your car with a personalized registration plate? Forget it: these days you have to have a 'cherished number'.

That's the term used by the Driver & Vehicle Licencing Agency in its number-plate auctions. Recently remodelled from a civil service department into a commercially-minded agency, the DVLA has naturally adopted the gimcrack language of modern marketing. It is no coincidence that the verb 'to cherish' is also a favourite of those who advertise the sort of 'heirlooms' and 'collectors' items' that come over in container ships from China.

To say that these number plates, bits of crockery and pewter models of the *Starship Enterprise* are 'to cherish' is to suggest that they are not simply there to be acquired, used or even enjoyed. It means they are there to be loved, and in a particularly intense way.

To 'cherish' comes from the French *chérir*, 'to hold dear'. Since its arrival in English in the fourteenth century, it has usually implied physical tenderness: for your spouse, or for small children, or fluffy kittens. In the Bible, for instance, King David is unsuccessfully 'cherished' on his deathbed by Abishag, a young Shunammite virgin, who is asked to lie with him to give him 'heat': a service not yet available on the NHS.

We also speak of 'cherished ideas', 'cherished friendships', and 'cherished institutions', meaning those we love and wish to nurture. Inanimate objects can be 'cherished', but have to have acquired an emotional resonance: landscapes, houses, musical instruments. Vehicle registration numbers hardly qualify.

The gift of a strip of metal and plastic bearing the number 'UR21' or 'BIG1' may create happy associations for the lucky recipient. They will thus *become* 'cherished numbers'. But it is hard to see how they could be described as 'cherished' at the time of the sale.

Except, perhaps, by those contemplating the money they will bring in.

Churn

Whenever those working in the bright new industries of our day – satellite television, mobile phones, cable television – are gathered together, one deceptively bucolic word rings out. That word is 'churn'.

'Churn' is where people rent a dish or a telephone and then, as soon as they see the size of their bill, send it back – or throw it in the river. But the word acquires new uses all the time. Under John Major, people spoke of 'churn' in Government, meaning people coming and going from the Cabinet.

For all this modernity, the word is fundamentally agricultural. A 'churn', obviously, is a vessel used in the making of butter. 'To churn' is to agitate milk or cream in such a vessel. The words are nearly one thousand years old in English, and come from the Common Teutonic *cirn*.

Since the seventeenth century, we have occasionally come across other liquids being 'churned', notably blood and sea water. In our own century we have had the expression 'to churn out', which is to produce literature, music or art mechanically, without waiting for inspiration.

The new usage seems to have originated in Wall Street. *American Speech*, the journal of the American Dialect Society, noted in 1955 that 'churning' was used to describe the practice of buying and selling large volumes of stock with little or no change in price.

Our own financial services sector adapted this during the 1980s, when a practice known as 'churn and burn' was widespread. This meant persuading customers to move their investments around, solely for the commission you would earn on each transaction.

Is it too fanciful to suggest that some of those sharp-suited salesmen flogging pensions and insurance subsequently moved on to more technological industries? And brought their charmingly evocative vocabulary with them?

Classic

'Oh, classic!' people say, when you've told them some anecdote about a mutual friend in an embarrassing situation. He might, for instance, have pranged his 'classic' Ford Capri while enraged by some 'classic' gaffe on Classic FM.

The word 'classic', used as an adjective, means 'excellent'. But it also means 'typical' or 'standard'. This ambiguity has been especially exploited by advertisers, who apply the word to boring things to give them a bogus air of quality.

In origin, 'classic', like 'classical', is simply an adaptation of the Latin adjective *classicus*, which meant 'of a high social class'. In English, from the seventeenth century, both words were used to describe the authors considered appropriate for reading and imitation in schools.

Naturally, these authors wrote in Latin and Greek, which all schoolchildren could read in the days when no one knew anything about education. So the words 'classical' and 'classic' came to be applied to those literatures, languages and eras.

Later, the word 'classical' was used to encompass the supposed formal perfection of the arts of that era, to the detriment of anything more contemporary, for instance Romanticism. By extension, the most 'perfect' era of anything else, from science to music, came to be known as its 'classical' period, and its artefacts known as 'classics'.

The 'classic blouse' was introduced by the tailor Weatherall's in the 1930s, and from that point the adjective came to imply that an object conformed to some sort of Platonic ideal above and beyond mere fashion or popularity.

This noble vision is now routinely applied to clapped-out cars from the Austin Allegro era, repeats of unfunny comedy series, and supermarket biscuits. Here it tends to mean the boring sort, say Nice or Rich Tea, without so much as a layer of chocolate to distract from their 'classic' biscuity nature.

Client

For a while, we were all supposed to be 'customers', whether we were standing on a railway platform waiting for a train or lying on a trolley in a hospital corridor waiting for a bed. Increasingly, though, everyone's a 'client'.

The distinction is that a 'client' uses someone's professional services rather than buying his products. It is supposed to sound classy – hence its appeal to hairdressers and estate agents – although it has actually been sliding down the social scale for hundreds of years.

In the fifteenth century, only lawyers had 'clients'. Later it was money-lenders. Today, a flick through the newspapers finds the word used of those who employ the services of architects, therapists, advertising agents, financial advisers, insurance brokers, theatrical and literary agents, PR people, midwives and even funeral directors. Truly, there is no escape.

Interestingly, for those who value historical resonances, the word has its origins in an ancient protection racket. The Romans used the original word, *cliens*, to describe those plebeians who sheltered under the patronage of a particular patrician. In return for the patron's protection and the promise of a peaceful life, the 'client' would pay through the nose. How very unlike our own relations with the valued professionals listed above.

In Middle English, the word seems to have meant variously 'a vassal', 'a hanger-on' or 'a dependent'. This last provides an interesting subtext to its adoption, in mid-twentieth century, as a more respectful way of describing those unfortunates requiring the assistance of social workers. Previously they were known, at least in Britain, as 'cases'.

Those misled into thinking that being called a 'client' is a mark of respect should always remember that it is what prostitutes call their customers. When they are being polite.

Compliant

Are you 'compliant'? No, neither am I. But being 'compliant' is rapidly becoming essential for modern life.

Recently, it has tended to mean 'Year 2000-compliant' or 'Millennium-compliant'. Whole companies, and not just individual bits of software, have had to promise that they wouldn't fall apart at the turn of the century.

But that's just the start. Products have to be 'compliant' with other products and with endless standards and rules. Firms must promise 'compliance' with all manner of regulations and ethical codes. Not for nothing is the football authorities' 'compliance officer' known as the 'sleazebuster'.

And yet, 'compliant' is the word we use of someone too easily persuaded, morally weak: the Vicar of Bray, for instance.

There's an obvious contradiction here, but neither of these meanings was there at the beginning. When the verb 'to comply', from the Italian *complire*, arrived at the beginning of the seventeenth century, it simply meant 'to be courteous'.

Hamlet, for instance, promises to 'comply with' the travelling players, shortly before he humiliates them. Later, though, the verb's meaning changed from 'being agreeable' to 'agreeing'.

The adjective 'compliant', meanwhile, meant 'civil' or 'well-mannered', but by the time of the Civil War, it had started to hint at obsequiousness. 'Compliance', too, came to suggest an unworthy lack of principle, particularly in matters of religion, with 'compliants', or compromisers, particularly scorned.

So where did our modern 'compliant' come from? Although almost all the early meanings of 'to comply' have disappeared, one has survived. Used of objects, it means 'to adapt itself' or 'to fit', just as 'compliant' people and things do today.

Here's an example from 1676: 'If the corks are steep'd in scalding water . . . they will comply better with the mouth of the bottle.' Those charged with proving that they are 'compliant' with everything from the calendar to the Data Protection Act will know the feeling.

Conservative

The word 'conservative' is a good one upon which to base a political party, because its connotations are usually good. A 'conservative' estimate is a sensible one. A 'conservative' shirt won't frighten your in-laws. A 'conservative' approach to a gamble won't cost you that shirt.

In this sense, 'conservative' is a synonym for 'cautious', a nuance first heard in the early years of this century. But that was before anyone had heard of Margaret Thatcher.

The word itself comes from the verb 'to conserve', from the Latin *conservare*, meaning to 'hold together'. But that was before anyone had heard of Mr Major.

The adjective 'conservative' first appeared in English in the fourteenth century, to mean something with *preservative* qualities, such as formaldehyde. And that was before anyone had heard of William Hague.

In Chaucer's unfinished *House of Fame*, the goddess Fame lives in a place described as 'most conservatyf the soun', which, in context, means something like 'conducive to the sound of applause'. Today's equivalent would be an appearance at the Tory party conference, especially if waving a Union Flag and brandishing instruments of torture.

In the nineteenth century, the word acquired its political meaning, as a label for what had been called the Tory Party, or at least for its less reactionary elements, headed by Sir Robert Peel. Previously a policy of keeping things the same was known as 'conservatory': later that would be used to describe a type of greenhouse.

First proposed in an article of January 1830, 'Conservative' was rapidly embraced. The old 'Tory', meanwhile, with its obscure origin as a name for gangs of Irish rebels fighting Oliver Cromwell, was cast aside after one hundred and fifty years. For some reason, this action seems faintly symbolic of the activities of 'conservatives' ever since.

Consultant

There are two ways to become a 'consultant'. You can spend years working impossible shifts, taking impossible exams and dealing with impossible people before reaching the top in hospital medicine. Or you can sell double glazing.

Until comparatively recently, most 'consultants' were medical men. Senior doctors have been known as 'consultants' (or 'consultant surgeons', 'consultant psychiatrists' and so on) since the late nineteenth century. Before that they were known as 'consulting physicians'.

Semantically speaking, 'consultant' or 'consulting physician' would seem to suggest someone who 'consults' other people, in the sense of asking their advice. In fact, the 'consultant' is the one who gives the advice, since he already knows everything. Or acts as if he does.

This linguistic curiosity can be explained. The ultimate source of both 'consultant' and 'consulting' in this sense is not the verb 'to consult' but the French verb *consulter*, which once meant to provide 'counsel' or professional advice.

The doctors did not keep 'consultant' to themselves for very long. As early as Sherlock Holmes, the word was a jocular synonym for private detective. And 'consultant' or 'consulting' engineers have been with us since the beginning of this century.

As currently used, it tends to means an independent practitioner who offers advice to a number of clients: but not all 'consultants' belong to traditional professions. Recent sightings include a 'sculpture consultant', a 'lactation consultant', and a 'bridal & wedding consultant'.

There are also companies which avoid their responsibilities as employers by operating through self-employed 'consultants'. It is also a favourite euphemism for those who sell things, often on commission only, but dislike the word 'sales'.

Radio Four's *Face The Facts* once exposed a firm selling a bogus 'cure' for depression at an extortionate price. The treatment was invented by a former double-glazing salesman – but it was peddled by 'consultants'.

Cool

Cool

No sooner had the incoming Labour Government discovered 'Cool' than it started disowning it. But the word will probably survive this disgrace: indeed, it will probably thrive on it. Ask any six-year-old.

'Cool' means anything from 'excellent' and 'highly fashionable' to 'all right, I suppose', depending on context and tone of voice. Amazingly, for those who remember when it was as embarrassing as 'heavy!' or 'far out!', it is now quite free of irony.

Both 'cool' and 'cold' have existed for at least a thousand years, but 'cool' has always been less unpleasant. By the fifteenth century, it had become a term of approval when applied to a person, suggesting calm and restraint, as it does today.

But the fashionable 'cool' comes from jazz. In the 1920s and 1930s, jazz was 'hot': fast, passionate and largely free of intellectual content. Then, in the late 1940s, a rival movement emerged, playing difficult music in a controlled, unemotional manner. Charlie Parker's 1947 'Cool Blues' expressed the mood. As early as 1948, the exclamation 'Cool!' was being used to express approval.

In the drug scene of the 1960s and 1970s, to be 'cool' was to appear in control despite being under the influence, or to have temporarily divested yourself of illegal drugs when 'busted' by the 'fuzz'. Now the preoccupations of that era are fashionable again, so is the slang – or some of it.

But what of 'Cool Britannia'? This was originally the title of a 1967 song by the Bonzo Dog Doo-Dah Band, satirizing the swinging London of an earlier Labour Prime Minister, Harold Wilson. Then, in 1996, Ben & Jerry revived it for a flavour of ice cream.

Soon it was everywhere. But those who used it as a label for London's brief moment in the sun had obviously never heard the song, which declared, with some justice, 'Cool Britannia, Britannia takes a trip / Britons never, never, never shall be hip'.

Core

'We can supply winkles,' says whelk stall man. 'But we do not consider them "core".'

The fashionable adjective 'core', usually used in such contexts as 'core values' and 'core business', means no more than 'central'. But it appeals to modern business, sounding both technological and caringly organic.

Clearly, it is a metaphor, but of what? Soft fruit? Geology? Nuclear physics? Originally, early in the fifteenth century, the word referred to the squeaky, seed-laden inner part of an apple. Ancient superstition had it that the 'core' of the fruit from the tree of knowledge stuck in Adam's throat, giving him the 'Adam's apple' as a reminder of his sin. A 'core' was thus something nasty, for instance the hard lump in the centre of a boil.

As your corporate relations department will tell you, this would not be the ideal way to characterize the central part of your business. But our modern 'core' has a later source. In the seventeenth century, it became the word for what was previously known as the 'heart' of a tree. From then on, 'core' increasingly referred to the valuable central parts of things, from ropes to nuclear reactors.

Abstractions arrived in the twentieth century, thanks to the efforts of archaeologists. They identified what they called 'core cultures', societies which made tools by chipping away at a lump of flint and retaining the middle part. The alternative, where the flint chips were used, was called a 'flake culture'.

Speaking of which, it was in California in 1935 that educationalists invented the 'core curriculum', followed by 'core vocabularies', 'core staff', 'core time' and more. Education has been one of the sources for the burgeoning vocabulary of business.

Today, management gurus invariably advise companies to concentrate on their 'core activities' – except when they are advising them to diversify into lots of others.

Counsellor

Once, if you'd advised someone to see a 'counsellor' they'd have gone straight to the Town Hall, where a local politician would have listened to their marital problems in bafflement. These days we know better.

The confusion between 'council' and 'counsel' goes back to the Romans. Normally very organized, they were lax enough on this occasion to use two virtually identical words. *Concilium* meant a meeting. *Consilium*, on the other hand, meant an advisory body.

When the words came into English they became hopelessly confused, with spellings like 'counseil' (in at least forty variants) and 'counceil' (fifteen variants) used indiscriminately.

Only in the sixteenth century was there an attempt to clarify things. 'Council' became either kind of body, deliberative or advisory, while 'counsel' became advice or the action of offering it. A 'counsellor' is really someone who gives advice, from Jesus Christ down, as those who know the *Messiah* will recall. It is still used in approximately this sense in the diplomatic service and in the courts in some of the United States, where it replaces the British 'counsel'.

Modern counselling, however, was mentioned first in the *Journal of Consulting Psychology* in 1940, where it was used to describe a new form of psychotherapy. Rejecting the detachment of the Freudian psychoanalyst, who likes to keep mum, this 'counsellor' would provide interpretation and emotional support, though rarely anything as straightforward as advice.

These days, everyone's a counsellor, from the person who helps you sort out your marriage to the one who helps you sort out your debts. 'Counsellors' deal with drugs, alcohol, sexual obsession and stress. They can tell you how to live with HIV and what colour lipstick to wear.

The apotheosis of the counselling trend came in the 1995 Kobe earthquake in Japan, where in the chaos people were left to sleep on the ground. They were, however, offered counselling.

Crack

If a friend tells you that he's going to some nightspot for 'the crack', how should you respond? Call the police? Or ask to join him?

Well, it is possible that he's looking for the well-known drug made by mixing cocaine and baking powder in a microwave oven. But more likely, he's using the Irish expression meaning everything from 'fun, games and practical jokes' to 'a good chat'.

'The crack' has been everywhere in the last few years, part of a wave of cheerful Oirishry. Shamrocks and green paint are the lingua franca of fun from Minnesota to Moscow, and Britain's brewing conglomerates would rather promote anyone's drinking customs than our own.

'The crack' is an Irish word, *craic*, usually translated as 'conversation'. It seems to have come from lowland Scots rather than Gaelic. The Scots have used 'crack' to mean news, chat, jokes and boasting since the fifteenth century.

There are lots of similar idioms in English. A 'crack regiment' is one worth boasting about, as is a 'cracking meal' or the 'cracker' you've shared it with. The colloquial expression 'to crack on' means to boast in a misleading way: 'He cracked on that he lived above a crack den, but we didn't believe him.'

A 'crack', meanwhile, is any kind of joke or barbed comment. And there's a lingering and noisy association with the act of breaking wind.

All these expressions stem from the Teutonic of our Continental forebears, who had a verb, sounding not unlike 'crack', that represented the noise of a dry stick breaking.

Undoubtedly, some things 'crack' quietly. It is from them that we get the various figurative expressions for mental disorder: 'cracked' and 'to crack up'.

Mostly, though, anything to do with the word 'crack' is likely to be noisy. Even the drug takes its name from the sound it makes while it's being cooked up.

Customer

In the last years of British Rail, it decided that those struggling with its services should be known as 'customers' rather than passengers. It thought it was being modern and responsive. Everyone else suspected a plot.

If everyone is a 'customer', mused the conspiracy theorists on the 7.53, BR is hardly obliged to run trains at all. It might as well stick to what it does best, which is being Tie Rack's landlord.

Now, as you know, British Rail has gone. But its 'customers' are still there, and they don't like the word any better. It invites cynicism, just as it does every time you enter a shop with a sign saying, 'The Customer Is Always Right' or, worse, 'The Customer Is King'. The bigger the promise, the worse the service.

As usual, our uneasiness about a word intended to flatter proves to have a solid historical basis. The current sense of the word arrived in the fifteenth century. A 'customer' is someone who takes his 'custom', or regular patronage, to the same shop. 'Custom' comes from a Latin original: *consuetudo*, meaning habit.

But 'customer' has connotations of its own. Consider such expressions as 'ugly customer' and 'awkward customer', which go back as far back as the Elizabethans. These are not shoppers whose left feet are bigger than their right: they are disreputable people.

A 'customer' in this sense is someone whose demeanour you feel 'accustomed to': 'I know your type,' you might say. It is used about criminals, dangerous animals and unexploded bombs.

In Shakespeare, interestingly, a 'customer' sometimes means a prostitute. 'I marry her? What! A customer?' sneers Cassio of Bianca, 'a courtezan', in *Othello*. We no longer have that sense, but that doesn't mean we like the word any better.

On the whole, the railway companies might have done better to stick with 'passenger'.

Czar

The news that Tony Blair wanted to appoint a 'czar' came as a surprise to those who remembered when many in the Labour Party were more enthusiastic about Lenin.

But this 'czar', whose job is to fight drugs, has nothing much to do with Russia. The title is an import from America, as its spelling indicates.

In Britain, we normally use 'tsar', a more accurate representation of the sound of the Cyrillic letter that starts the Russian word. The spelling 'czar' dates back to the sixteenth century but was replaced in Western Europe by the late nineteenth, when *The Times* opted for 'tsar'. America stuck to the old version.

But what has all this to do with the fight against narcotics? 'Czar' was the formal title of the king or emperor of Russia, first adopted by Ivan III at the end of the fifteenth century. It was a cut-down version of an earlier word, *tsisari*, a Slavonic version of 'Caesar'.

A 'czar' or 'tsar' is an absolute ruler. Its current political vogue stems from the ironical use of the term in nineteenth-century America when, it should be noted, the real Tsar was still alive and well. There is a humorous reference to the president as the 'Czar uv all the Amerikas' as early as 1866.

Later, all manner of minor tyrants were awarded the same title: union leaders, industrialists, sports bosses. This was because 'czar' fits a headline, whereas 'president', 'chief executive' – and 'anti-drug co-ordinator' – do not.

In 1970, the *Guardian* reported that 'many Presidents establish a staff "czar" to cut down on "unnecessary" memos and contacts'. It is from this that the current spate of 'czars' stems.

President Clinton's first 'drug czar' found absolute power absolutely awful, and went off to teach sociology. Let us hope his British equivalent has better luck.

Denial

In the long-running backstage farce that dominated Bill Clinton's second White House term, 'denial' was for a long time the word on everyone's lips.

It was a 'denial' that the President was accused of demanding from Monica Lewinsky when a court started examining his sexual history. It was a 'denial' he was making when he went red in the face and started jabbing his finger at reporters.

Ms Lewinsky, however, should have seen this coming. She had already complained to a friend – and the friend's hidden tape recorder – that the President was 'in denial' about the affair.

The difference is this. A 'denial' is a refusal to admit to others that something has happened. To be 'in denial' is to refuse to admit it to yourself.

The word 'denial' has special resonances in Washington. Thanks to the doctrine of 'deniability' developed in the Reagan era, the President can safely 'deny' any action of which he has no direct knowledge. The President's advisers therefore arrange all manner of actions on precisely that basis.

This did not, evidently, apply to the action in which President Clinton and Ms Lewinsky were involved. Mr Clinton could hardly have had more direct knowledge. His denial had to be a lie.

Ms Lewinsky, however, maintained that he was 'in denial', meaning his conscious mind was avoiding the problem by refusing to accept its existence. That would make The Leader of the Free World not so much bad as mad, more victim than villain. But then, the poor girl was besotted.

Big-haired American women, trained on daytime television, instinctively turn to psychobabble in times of crisis, and increasingly we do the same. 'Denial' is one of the 'ego-defence mechanisms' identified in Freud's *The Psychopathology of Everyday Life*, written at the turn of the twentieth century.

Freud thought that anxiety was the source of denial. We know, however, that it is Lake Victoria.

Directional

When you read that a new outfit is 'directional', what are you to assume? That it only achieves its optimum effect when viewed from the front?

Or perhaps it means that it conducts electricity in one direction only? Or that it emits a beam of radio signals along a compass bearing?

All are acceptable definitions of the word 'directional'. But none has anything to do with the way the word is used in fashion, a mysterious world at the best of times.

The fashion 'directional', which emerged in the 1980s, is a term of approbation rather than description. It tells us that an outfit or a designer has 'edge' or 'a sense of the Zeitgeist'. Does that help?

The standard 'directional' is the adjectival form of 'direction', a sixteenth-century borrowing of the French *direction*. 'Direction' originally meant instructions or orders: the act whereby someone or something was placed on a particular course. Later, it was more commonly used for the course itself.

The adjective 'directional' came into its own in the nineteenth century when engineers used it in the context of moving electric currents, sound waves and the like. It is still used about those aerials, microphones, and loudspeakers which only achieve their desired effect when pointed in a particular direction. The same may be true of some items of clothing, but that isn't what the fashion 'directional' is about.

In that world, the adjective seems to describe designs which 'have a sense of direction' and are confident and daring. It also seems to imply that the outfit will provide its wearers with a 'direction' otherwise lacking in their sad little lives.

It is worth noting that in France, home of fashion, *la direction* still has its authoritarian edge: it means guidance, or 'the management'.

Which may be why a 'directional' outfit is not so much one you wear, as one that wears you.

Diversity

If you go for a job and are asked whether you are in favour of 'diversity', try not to ask, 'Of what?'

'Diversity' is a code-word. It's the new term for what were until recently called 'equal opportunities' or 'anti-discrimination' policies.

Inevitably, this is a concept from the US, where it has been enthusiastically embraced by private and public sectors alike. Here's a statement on the subject from the computer company IBM, once a byword for sinister technocratic uniformity, now reinventing itself as sharing, caring and diverse.

'We the people at IBM are first and foremost individuals,' it declares. 'Individuals in every sense of the word. We come from diverse origins, live different lifestyles and pursue our own dreams. What we share is the belief that each and every one of us makes a meaningful contribution to IBM.'

How touching. Whereas 'equal opportunities' and 'anti-discrimination' involved imposing on the workplace an idea of social justice, 'diversity' seems to be about using the different individuals who make up your workforce as assets to gain advantage in a multicultural world. Less pious, more commercial – and very New Labour.

The word 'diversity' has been with us since the fourteenth century, meaning much the same as it does now: difference or variousness. This is slightly odd, since in the Old French and Latin from which the English word emerged it meant wickedness, perversity or disagreement.

In our century, 'diversity' has mostly had scientific uses. The 'diversity factor' is a measure in electricity generation equipment. In radio, 'diversity reception' is a system for using different aerials to receive a fading radio station (not a reference to BBC Radio Three).

It is not surprising that employers prefer 'diversity' to 'equal opportunities'. It sounds modern, responsive and socially concerned – and commits them to almost nothing.

Dumb

It's usually the BBC that sets people off. 'It's "dumbing down",' they say, turning down their mouths to show that they consider it a distasteful expression – but sadly appropriate.

'Dumbing down' gained prominence in 1995 when it was the title of a book about the collapse of American education. Here it is used by those – and there are many of us – who want to know why Radio Three now has a 'celebrity panel game'.

In the US, 'dumb' means stupid. Only as an afterthought do American dictionaries record that 'dumb' also means 'lacking the power of speech', explaining nervously that it is 'often offensive when applied to humans'.

British dictionaries, meanwhile, state without apology that 'dumb' means 'unable to speak'. Only then do they add that it can mean stupid.

How can the same word be so different on opposite sides of the Atlantic? Perhaps because it is not quite the same word. The American 'dumb' is, at the very least, heavily influenced by the Dutch *dom* and German *dumm*, both of which *do* mean stupid.

Before English, German and Dutch evolved, these words had a common ancestor. It would have sounded something like 'dumb' and meant 'unable to engage in conversation'.

The Anglo-Saxons, living across the water, kindly reserved the word for those unable or unwilling to speak, saying nothing about their intelligence. That's the British version. The early Germans also used the word for the stupid – and, for good measure, the deaf.

In modern German, however, and in Dutch, deaf and mute have gone, leaving only stupid. But those languages were common in nineteenth-century America, and that's when their meaning fastened itself to the English word.

In 1941, when the 'stupid' sense was still rare here, Walt Disney conjured up a shy and apparently none-too-bright elephant. He called it *Dumbo*, and soon there was no escape.

Edge

Whether you're promoting magazines, frocks or a range of scatter cushions, it's vital that they should have 'edge', the mysterious quality that makes a thing sharp, aggressive and attractively dangerous.

It was ever thus. In the era of *Beowulf*, twelve hundred years or so ago, the only 'edge' was the cutting blade of a sword. To have 'edge', in the rhetoric of the Middle Ages, was to have a lot of bloodthirsty swordsmen at your command. You don't get more sharp, aggressive or dangerous than that.

Only at the end of the sixteenth century was 'edge' used figuratively, to mean strength or 'keenness' in emotion or argument. But it has stayed with us ever since. Consider Wodehouse's *Psmith, Journalist* of 1915, in which the title character notes that being hit over the head by a blunt instrument 'will give our output precisely the edge it requires'. Today he'd be working for Roger Cook.

Business people, meanwhile, who talk about getting 'an edge', meaning an advantage, are using an American expression from the 1920s. But the clash of broadswords still lurks in the background. The same goes for the ubiquitous 'cutting-edge', meaning 'advanced' or 'forward-looking'.

'Leading-edge', however, is slightly less aggressive. It still means 'in the forefront', but it derives from the front end of a propeller or an aircraft wing rather than from military cutlery.

Sadly, those who struggle to develop 'edge', or achieve 'an edge', are in danger of going 'over the edge': cracking up, or going mad. Here a different metaphor comes into play.

Since the fourteenth century, the word 'edge' has also meant 'the boundary of a surface'. The surface in this case is the flat earth of normality on which we all attempt to stand. To go 'over the edge' is to sail towards the horizon before falling into nothingness, or worse. Mind how you go.

Elders

Local authorities love euphemisms. In one London borough, sweeping the streets is now called 'Streetcare'. Help for the blind and the deaf is provided by 'Sensory Impairment Services'. And the old and confused are offered tea and sympathy at something called 'Elders First'.

It could be worse. 'Elders' beats 'senior citizens' or 'seniors', which is what Americans call those entering their 'golden years'. And it is kinder than 'oldies', 'wrinklies' or 'twirlies', a nickname coined by bus conductors, tired of being asked, 'Can I use my free pass now, or am I *too early?*'

The word 'elders' has some of the dignity that ought to accompany old age, being old itself. It appears in *Beowulf*, the Anglo-Saxon epic. It also has connotations of wisdom and leadership.

Originally 'elder' was the normal comparative form of the adjective 'old'. Then the word 'older' arrived, leaving 'elder' to the minor task of differentiating between family members of different ages. The expression 'elder statesmen', meanwhile, comes from Japan. It is an approximate translation of *Genro*, a group of wise old men who advised the emperor at the end of the nineteenth century.

Unlike 'older', however, 'elder' is also a noun. Used mainly in the plural, it originally meant a person's parents, ancestors or predecessors. Then it meant anyone older than the person using it, and finally, by Shakespeare's time, it had come to mean any old person at all.

In the King James Bible it is used for those who lead a community, by virtue of their age. Later it was used by various churches to describe both clergy and lay officials. Indeed, in parts of the US, 'elder' is used for clergymen of any denomination, however bogus.

In this religious context it is interesting to note that an 'elder' is also a type of tree: the tree from which Judas Iscariot is said to have hanged himself.

Empower

Rich and poor, managers and staff, parents, consumers and job-seekers, we have all spent the last few years either 'empowering' ourselves or having 'empowerment' thrust upon us. It doesn't make us any more powerful – but it might make us *feel* as if we are.

That's because 'to empower' has acquired a rather specialized meaning. In the seventeenth century, when it appeared, it meant simply 'to give power to someone'. The Crown and Church authorities would 'empower' their subordinates to raise an army, or open a school. Later, it was used less specifically. God, for example, was said to 'empower' those who believed in him – as was the Devil.

Our modern reflexive verb comes from the radical feminists, who spent much of the 1970s sitting on beanbags discussing power. It was obviously a male thing. Should they abolish it – or seize it?

The approved answer was to spread it around: to 'empower' everyone. The 'empowerment' beloved of contemporary management is a distorted reflection of that: managers 'empower' their subordinates by letting them decide their own priorities, though rarely their own salaries. This has the advantage that those empowered can take the blame when things go wrong.

The feminists, meanwhile, found that awarding power to people was all too patronizing: besides, they had little to give. Instead they could help people 'empower' themselves, which is to say, develop their own psychological resources and self-respect.

This 'personal power' is the theme of thousands of inspirational books, from *The Power of Positive Thinking* (1952) to *Awaken Your Inner Power* (1995). All insist that this personal power, unlike the seventeenth-century version, has nothing to do with controlling or dominating other people.

In other words, to 'empower oneself' is not really about gaining power: it's about losing the feeling of powerlessness.

Enterprise

Strange to tell, but the ancient University of Cambridge now provides a home for something called The Margaret Thatcher Chair of Enterprise Studies. How quickly our ancient institutions have come to love transatlantic jargon: and the universities haven't been far behind either.

'Enterprise' is a would-be glamorous replacement for the mundane 'business' or 'sales'. People now read 'enterprise studies' at university before taking jobs as 'enterprise professionals' in 'enterprise organizations'.

These compound nouns were unknown in Britain before the Thatcher era, which at least means she has earned the Cambridge honour. Before that, 'enterprise' stood alone, often against the world. An 'enterprise', adopted from French in the fifteenth century, was an undertaking, usually involving something daring and warlike.

Later it came to mean the quality of spirit necessary for conquest, piracy and circumnavigating the globe in a leaky boat. Flattering though the comparison might seem, this is not precisely the same quality that is required in those selling life assurance or photocopiers.

By the middle of the nineteenth century, however, the word 'enterprise' was already being used in relation to more sedate activities, for instance running companies. And companies themselves began to be called 'enterprises', especially in America.

In 1979, the Thatcher Government began importing American political ideas, including the 'enterprise zone', an area of land where property developers were bribed to build empty warehouses. Soon we were said to be living in an 'enterprise culture', although that rarely made it easier to get a decent plumber.

Now the word is moving on. Following the American pattern, companies are dividing themselves between the heroic 'enterprise departments', who sell things, and 'back office', who do everything else.

If this is the way of the future, though, it is a mystery why aliens encountering the USS *Enterprise* tend to go for their weapons – rather than their chequebooks.

Euro

As a name for a product, 'Euro' isn't at all bad. It's bright, bouncy, optimistic: ideal for a small hatchback or a chocolate bar.

This time, it's attached to something more complicated: the common European currency, and with that our national destiny. But the name itself is fine. Rather than the rubbish the 'branding consultants' would have given us – Corus, Diageo, Egg – the polyglot bureaucrats have spawned something attractive.

For a start, it's a lot less ambiguous than some other names of currencies. You won't be able to buy a 'Euro' of potatoes, have your car locked in a 'Euro', nor 'Euro' somebody's head in. And it sounds friendly, perhaps because it ends in 'o', like Lego, Brio, Polo, Giro and a whole string of baby words.

On the announcement of the currency's name, the then Prime Minister John Major told newspapers that he 'would have preferred a more dignified name . . . with some history behind it'. But how much history, exactly?

'Euro' comes from *Eüropë*, which was introduced by Homer, about eight centuries before Christ. Meaning 'the wide place', it meant first mainland Greece, then Greece's back garden behind it, and then the whole continental shooting-match – which is what, until the last few years, it has always been.

The coin is trying to symbolize the united aspirations of a continent that has been divided since time began. It must not mean more to one nation than another. *Eüropë* is the name of a goddess, mentioned in the earliest Greek myths. She is not some here today, gone tomorrow politician, like Jean Monnet or Charlemagne.

We already have 'Euro-' words, as you will have noticed. We have 'Eurovision' and 'Eurostar', 'Eurodollar', 'Euroflora', 'Eurojet' and hundreds more. This may not say anything about the merits of the European single currency, but it does show that people like the sound of 'Euro'.

Excluded

'In those days,' a clergyman said recently, 'I would have called them "the poor". But now I know to call them "the excluded".'

'The poor' is good enough for the King James Bible, where it appears no fewer than one hundred and forty-two times. But contemporary Christianity speaks the language of our day. It is 'non-judgemental', and it is euphemistic.

To 'exclude' is to shut out: from the Latin *exclaudere*, meaning just that. 'Excluded' is also the modern jargon for 'expelled from school'.

The Government's contribution has been the 'social exclusion unit', which deals with those 'excluded' from society. By this it means The People Previously Known As The Poor.

Academics invented the concept of the 'excluded' so that they could get over the fact that many of the poor in a modern Western society are not, in a material sense, all that poor at all. Reasons advanced for their 'exclusion' include health, race, religion, language and geography, although not, as yet, having been to the wrong school.

For politicians, the 'excluded' have tremendous advantages over 'the poor'. To help the poor, you tend to have to give them money. You can assist the 'excluded' by giving them a bit of advice.

Academics and researchers, meanwhile, have discovered that the ideal way to assist 'the excluded' is to spend a few days in a conference hall to which they have not been invited. 'Social exclusion' has thus become a hot topic on the circuit, gradually replacing more meaning-ful subjects such as poverty and unemployment.

The thing about the verb 'to exclude' is that it needs a subject: someone to do the shutting out. No doubt these academics, research-ers and politicians look dispassionately at the question of who is to blame for the plight of the people concerned.

But the term 'excluded' has already made up its mind. Somebody else is.

Experience

Experience

A child comes home from school clutching a leaflet about a forth-coming school trip. On the front are the words 'Experience Our Animals'. Below that is a picture of a leopard.

How exactly does a five-year-old 'experience' a leopard? And what if the leopard objects?

Once it was enough to say you had *seen* the Lions of Longleat. But now you can see and hear everything by staring at a glass screen. People want to 'experience' things.

'Experience', from the Latin for 'a test' or 'a trial', suggests active participation. Which is why the Greenwich Dome exhibition will be known as The New Millennium Experience. You'll be in a queue, but it'll be a real queue.

In fourteenth-century English, 'an experience' was an experiment. 'Experience' was the wisdom that came from trying things out, or from some powerful event. Later, it came to mean the knowledge and expertise of a lifetime.

To the seventeenth-century Puritans, 'experience' became 'Experience', a powerful influx of religious feeling. To William Blake, writing his *Songs of Experience*, more than a century later, it was guilt and sin.

This type of 'experience', usually with 'sexual' in parentheses, was central to the 1960s, the era in which our leaders grew up. The Jimi Hendrix Experience weren't called that because their leader had been playing for a long time. The name implied both that Jimi was almost divinely inspired and that he was a very naughty boy. *Are You Experienced?*, the title of the group's first album, made it clear which was the more marketable.

Is it fanciful to see a connection between the Jimi Hendrix Experience and The New Millennium Experience, both known to initiates as 'The Experience' and both promising something life-changing and unforgettable?

Perhaps Mr Blair is going to give us a few tunes on his famous electric guitar.

Extreme

Idly reading the packaging of a set of razor blades, I was startled to discover that they were 'designed for extreme closeness and extreme comfort'.

'Extreme comfort'! Surely that's an oxymoron, I thought, as I attempted to staunch the flow of blood from my ear lobe. But that doesn't matter. It's only there because 'extreme' is a fashionable word.

You can tell, because Action Man, the playground favourite, now wears 'extreme shades'. Not fuchsia and lime green, but a trendy pair of sunglasses. And that's not even the 'extreme sports' model.

Those 'extreme sports' are undoubtedly the source of the word's vogue. The new name, along with clothes in bright colours, has revolutionized pursuits that were once the preserve of bearded men in cable-knit jumpers: rock-climbing, parachuting, hang-gliding, eating beef and anything else with an element of risk.

Attempts have been made to borrow the label for less risky pursuits. But a pair of roller skates looks no more exciting with 'extreme' written on the side. I have even seen an 'extreme' fishing rod.

In origin, 'extreme' is an adaptation of the Latin *extremus*, which means 'outermost' or 'farthest'. It is still used this way today. 'Look up there on the extreme right,' you might say, 'where that Lycra-clad rock-climber has just fallen off the cliff.'

The most common modern sense is that of being or doing something 'to the utmost degree'. This gave us 'extreme poverty', a phrase first used in 1475, when it meant more than not having a video. It is from this thin semantic branch that 'extreme comfort' dangles.

Sadly for my razor blades, the word has always been negative in its implications: it means 'excessive'. So while we can contemplate 'extreme heat' and 'extreme pain' and 'extreme cold', 'extreme comfort', like Action Man's 'extreme shades', is just silly.

This may, however, be an 'extreme' view.

Fatal

You are using your computer when a message appears on the screen: 'Fatal Error'. What should you do? Check your pulse to make sure you are still breathing? Step back from the machine? Or take a deep breath while you ponder what to do next?

The truth is, a 'fatal error' won't kill you. It won't even give you an electric shock. But it might make you want to weep.

It's not your mistake, but the software's. In a 'fatal error', the program starts doing a job, but can't complete it. Instead it gets half-way and stops dead. But anything you have been working on is likely to be lost. Hence the tears.

Irritating, then, but not what we usually mean by 'fatal'. A 'fatal' heart attack, for instance, is one that kills you, with no chance to click the 'restart' button.

Historically, however, 'fatal' has not always implied death. Introduced to English at the time of Chaucer, it meant 'decreed by fate'. But since fate tended to be on the unhelpful side, the word quickly came to mean 'doomed', before settling down as 'deadly' or 'irreversibly destructive'.

Since then, our tendency to exaggerate the awfulness of things has weakened it. We still talk of 'fatal accidents', but at the same time we are quite happy to say that it is 'fatal' to wear a white shirt when eating spaghetti.

For this development, some authorities have blamed the French, whose *fatal* lacks our word's seriousness. Consider the *femme fatale*, the kind of woman who lures men into 'fatal errors' undreamed of in the world's software houses.

Interestingly, 'fate' comes from the Latin noun *fatum*, meaning 'that which has been spoken'. One's fate was, literally, the sentence pronounced by the gods. Those who regularly use a personal computer will know the feeling.

Feelgood

The word 'feelgood' is a stranger to most dictionaries, but it's not hard to work out what it means. It describes something that provides 'a sense of well-being'.

Before becoming part of the vocabulary of politicians, it was common in the folksy language of American advertising, which would promise 'a feelgood eating experience', usually meaning something constructed in a laboratory out of industrial by-products.

The 'feelgood factor', the sense that things might be getting better, was the thing that was supposed to save the Major Government. From 1991, its appearance was endlessly predicted, but it proved elusive. In the end, the voters decided that if they couldn't feel good, they could always feel different, and elected someone else.

Before that there had been 'feelgood factors', in the plural. And in 1988, the then Labour leader Neil Kinnock, with his instinct for getting it half right, had been heard to complain that the Tories had been trying to create 'a feelgood feeling'. But 'feelgood factor' became the catchphrase.

'Feelgood' itself is obviously derived from 'Dr Feelgood', an expression with a long history in Black American culture. Famously, it provided a name for a British r'n'b band, who took it from a Piano Red song of 1962, 'Dr Feel-Good'.

But there was also an Aretha Franklin B-side of 1967: 'After one visit to Dr Feelgood you'll understand why Feelgood is his name.' Whatever Aretha was singing about, it doesn't seem to have had much to do with the Public Sector Borrowing Requirement.

The nickname 'Dr Feelgood' was subsequently bestowed on various political workers charged with conjuring the factor into existence: none succeeded. In any case it's a risky quip. In jazz slang, a 'Dr Feelgood' is someone who supplies illegal drugs to musicians.

Whether this is an appropriate analogy for the art of pleasing the electorate is for others to decide.

Fluffy

Eyebrows were raised when Newt Gingrich, the famously combative Speaker of the American House of Representatives, decided to become 'fluffy and co-operative'. But he was only catching the mid-1990s mood.

It was the era of *Four Weddings and a Funeral*, described by its star Hugh Grant as a 'British-made fluffy comedy'. Such films didn't depict our society but what Alicia Silverstone, star of the Californian *Clueless*, defined as a 'happy, nice, fluffy world'.

You can guess what 'fluffy' means. It means something is warm, appealing, likeable, even innocent. A stretch for Mr Gingrich, but worth a try.

'Fluff' is a late eighteenth-century word, meaning something light, feathery, loose and vaguely woolly that sticks to your clothes. It may have come from the earlier 'flue', the down of a rabbit. More likely, it's onomatopoeic, the word's soft consonants – voiceless labiodental fricatives, since you ask – reflecting the downy quality of 'fluff' itself.

The word has had many figurative meanings. Railway clerks in the nineteenth century were 'fluffing' when they short-changed passengers. Later, actors were said to 'fluff' their lines when they garbled or forgot them, and the word is still used about public mistakes, especially by sportsmen and musicians.

There is also 'a bit of fluff', meaning a young woman, first used in 1903 and still with us, a century of feminism notwithstanding.

But where is our contemporary 'fluffy'? The word has long been used as an affectionate synonym for 'silly'. There is a jolly A. P. Herbert rhyme of 1927, in which he says he likes his female friends: 'With fluffy complexions, like plums on a wall, / And fluffy opinions, and no brains at all.' And in the 1935 *Blandings Castle*, P. G. Wodehouse describes the Earl of Emsworth as 'a fluffy-minded and amiable old gentleman'.

A likeable quality, then, but perhaps not quite what Newt Gingrich had in mind.

Fluid

How 'fluid' everything seems these days. The economy, the market, the situation, government policy, the universe itself. No wonder no one knows what's going on.

It would be nice to say that this ubiquitous expression was a modern perversion of a venerable scientific term, but that wouldn't be true. The word has always been used figuratively as much as literally. Indeed, the Romans used *fluidus*, the Latin adjective from which fluid derives, in both ways. Literally, it meant flowing. Figuratively, it meant soft, slack and languid, qualities of which they disapproved.

The word 'fluid', and its abstract noun, 'fluidity', first arrived in English in Elizabethan translations. In those days translation seems not to have been the most demanding activity: when translators got stuck, they used the original word, contributing handsomely to the growth of English. John Florio's celebrated 1603 translation of Montaigne, for instance, simply incorporated the French *fluidité* as 'fluiditie', using it to describe a quality in prose style.

'Fluid' is still used to praise a flowing quality, in writing, musicianship, dance and even sport. But it has often suggested a less desirable uncertainty and unease. As early as 1672, the Vicar of Islington wrote about 'The fluid and transitory condition of man's life.' People in Islington still speak of little else.

Meanwhile, the noun 'fluid', first cited in 1661, has somehow come to sound faintly comical, even indecent. It has its genuine medical uses, in 'spinal fluid', 'cerebral fluid' and so on, but otherwise it carries a whiff of smut.

The source for this ubiquitous innuendo must be Stanley Kubrick's film *Dr. Strangelove* (1963), which featured an American general driven mad by the belief that the Russians were somehow poisoning Americans' 'precious bodily fluids'.

That alone was enough to push 'fluid' into that class of words (like 'Matron' or 'Penge') that it is difficult to say with a straight face.

Focus

This may be a short-sighted age, but it is very keen on 'focus'. 'Focus' is what every professional sportsman wants, what every New Age guru promises, what every last struggling plc fights to achieve.

And then there are the 'focus groups' setting the direction of our Government and, more worryingly, of Radio Four. Even the trusty Ford Escort has succumbed, replaced by the glamorous Ford Focus, whose name apparently reflects the role of 'focus groups' in its design.

Focus, as classicists will know, is Latin for fireplace. But when a sprinter says he's working on his 'focus' he doesn't mean he's taken up ornamental bricklaying.

In the late sixteenth century, people experimenting with lenses and mirrors needed a word for the point where the rays of light met to produce burning: the fire place, as it were. They used the Latin word, *focus*.

Later, as their optical work developed, 'focus' was also used for the point at which an object was seen clearly. Both ideas, of concentration and of clarity, fed the figurative uses that appeared in the nineteenth century, when people first began to 'focus' their thoughts.

Today 'focus' is a quality valued in 'personal development', the trendy discipline in which fire-breathing salesmen swap motivational tips with fire-walking mystics. In simple terms, it means learning to concentrate on what you're doing, rather than letting your mind drift to events in *The Archers* or the worrying rattle in your Ford Focus.

The 'focus group', meanwhile, is a marketing tool based on concentrating a group of demographically significant people in a room and inviting them to indulge in wide-ranging criticisms of other people's work. They usually oblige.

Those who swear by this curious process, however, should be aware that no 'focus group' ever created anything, except possibly a row.

Friendly

Friendly

'Friendly' is a nice word: cuddly, soft, incapable of aggression. Perhaps that's why it is so often used in such compounds as 'user-friendly' or 'environmentally-friendly', where it gives an air of benevolence to some frightening bit of technology or noxious chemical.

Computer makers pioneered this '-friendly' when they were trying to show that a mysterious box of electronics with a blank expression and a reputation for costing people their jobs was actually everyone's new best friend. A 'friendly, interactive keyboard' is recorded in the US as early as 1979.

The first '-friendly' compounds soon followed. An American article of 1981, for instance, nervously described the development of '"user friendly" systems that make it easier for the average worker to handle a laser'. These compounds mirrored a construction common in German: *kinderfreundlich*, for instance, is a direct translation of 'child-friendly'.

By the spring of 1982, such expressions as 'environment-friendly' were common enough in the States for the British *Economist* to be able to denounce them as 'abominations'. Nonetheless, they have established themselves here. Some years ago, 'dolphin-friendly' canned tuna arrived, bearing a promise that absolutely no dolphins were harmed in its production. 'Tuna-friendly' tuna, however, is still some way off.

The word 'friend' started life as the past participle of the Old Teutonic verb *frijojan*, meaning to love. It continues to evolve. Our own century has contributed a grim new twist.

In World War I, soldiers applied the adjective 'friendly' to their own shells, passing overhead or, sometimes, dropping disastrously short. In 1976, a book called *Friendly Fire* examined the phenomenon of American soldiers killed by their own artillery.

By the time of the 1991 Gulf War, the alliterative expression was everywhere, possibly because, by some accounts, more American troops were killed by their own weapons in that conflict than by those of the Iraqis. Not always such a nice word, then.

Full-on

What does it mean when you hear people say they are having a 'full-on relationship'? Or that they are planning a 'full-on good time'? Or when you read, as you now can, that a product will give you 'full-on beautiful hair'?

Previously, the only things that were 'full-on' were mechanical or electrical: your brakes as you skidded into a ditch, your headlights when you were flagged down in a built-up area, a tap spraying water all over your kitchen.

But this 'full-on', which apparently started among students in the Midlands, isn't about that. It's an intensifier, meaning something like 'all-out' or 'no holds barred', perhaps with a touch of recklessness or defiance.

Where did it come from? It sounds redolent of British dance culture of the late 1980s and early 1990s. But the first recorded appearance is in the name of a Canadian company, 'Full-On Design', founded in 1991 and specializing in writing slogans on motorcycle helmets. But did they really invent it? And how did it get here?

It may just be a modification of another 'full-' compound, some of which date back to the fourteenth century. It most resembles 'full-out', a synonym for 'flat-out', both sometimes used to express the idea of reckless enthusiasm. Or it may even have something to do with 'full-blown', a word usually heard only in the context of AIDS.

Alternately, it may just be an intensification of 'on'. To be 'on' has, at various times, meant to be eager, well informed, drunk and under the influence of drugs, which certainly seems to be in the right general area.

Surprisingly, the Victorians may be relevant here. According to Partridge's *Dictionary of Slang*, from about 1860 'full on for it (or one)' meant 'ready and extremely willing'. It also had 'an indelicate connotation'. Not an entirely new expression, then?

Geek

There was great excitement the day 'geek' made it into *The Times*. Not the newspaper, you understand, but the offices, where someone directed the word at the editor, shortly before resigning on the spot.

But what does it mean? A basic guess would suggest that a 'geek' is someone who relates better to computers than to people. A synonym for 'nerd', in fact. But this is an over-simplification.

For 'geek' has been 'reclaimed'. Wander about the dingier parts of the Internet and you will find many people – Americans, principally – who wear the 'geek' label with pride.

They include fantasy gamers, trekkies, neo-pagans and other self-proclaimed weirdos you'd prefer not to sit next to at a dinner party. But despite being social outcasts, they are all social with one another. That, they say, is how they differ from nerds.

But what has all this to do with the editor of *The Times*? Well, the word is really nothing to do with computers: it's a much older term of abuse.

In current American dictionaries, a 'geek' is defined as 'a person with an unusual or odd personality'. But older editions let slip that a 'geek' was once 'a carnival "wild man" whose act usually includes biting the head off a live chicken or snake'. Not too far removed from a newspaper editor, then.

'Geek' was an English dialect word before resurfacing in the US, although it was often spelt 'geck'. In Victorian Whitby, for instance, it was recorded as meaning 'a fool' or 'a dupe'.

It originally appeared in Britain from Low German in the sixteenth century, meaning both a gesture of derision and the person derided. Shakespeare used it in *Twelfth Night* and *Cymbeline*.

Directors of these difficult comedies are advised to use the modern pronunciation, thereby guaranteeing themselves at least one laugh.

Glamour

Glamour

Fashion has rediscovered 'glamour'! How many times have you read that? But beware: 'glamour' is not as innocent a word as it might appear.

'Glamour' is literally a spell cast on the eyes, making things look more beautiful than they really are. A reasonable description of the art of the cosmetics counter, you might say. But it also reminds us of the word's occult origins.

In the beginning, the word was about witchcraft. It is eighteenth century in origin, Scottish, and admirably defined in a book of 1721: 'When devils, wizards or jugglers deceive the sight, they are said to cast glamour o'er the eyes of the spectator.'

It started as a corruption of the Old French *gramaire*, which meant, on the face of it, nothing more suspicious than learning. But in the eyes of the uneducated, learning was invariably associated with necromancy and the occult. So *gramaire* gave us both 'grammar' and 'glamour'.

Sir Walter Scott was responsible for popularizing 'glamour' in its supernatural sense. Soon, however, it came to be used of beauty, particularly of the deceptive kind.

The modern use, to mean attractiveness or allure, is American. It started with the 1930s Hollywood expression 'glamour girl' and has maintained its stylish reputation. But among British photographers, especially those without film in their cameras, 'glamour' tends to mean 'nude'.

The occult aspects have never gone away, either. Aleister Crowley defined 'glamour' as 'duality in act, word and thought'. The New Age guru Alice A. Bailey used it to mean the mental fog in which we unenlightened people live.

She expounded this point of view in *Glamour – A world problem*, one of a long series of books telepathically dictated to her by DK, a Tibetan 'Master of Wisdom', between 1935 and 1945.

And you thought 'glamour' was just about hair and make-up.

Global

They say the world is shrinking. The word 'global' provides the proof.

An invitation to take on the 'global supervision' of a project should give you the chance to rack up your Air Miles – but it will probably mean more hours at your desk. A 'global memo' ought to cause a stir in San Diego and Ulan Bator: more likely, it will go to the people sitting on either side of you. All rather disappointing.

'Global' is really the French word *global*. They took the Latin *globus*, meaning a ball or sphere, and turned it into *globe*. In the sixteenth century, the Age of Discovery, we borrowed it for use in geometry and extended it to cover the spherical world.

Both languages struggled to come up with adjectives to mean 'globe-like'. The French tried *globulaire* and *globique*. We experimented with globar, globular, globoid, globed, globose, globate, globated, globous and, on rare occasions, even 'global'.

The French had *global*, too, but used it of 'round' figures and 'whole' concepts: it translates as 'total', 'gross' or 'overall', but never 'world'. *Capital global*, for instance, doesn't mean New York – or even Paris – but total capital.

At the end of the nineteenth century, the French adjective became established in English. As it did so, the specific meaning of the French word collided with the broader sense which English tried to give it: 'pertaining to the whole world'. It took the 'global war' of the 1940s for our version to dominate.

But the word's French heritage has not disappeared. Computer experts use the word that way: a 'global search' is a search through a whole document; a 'global message' is one that is sent round a computer network, however small.

And it is still important in business. Which is why, when your boss asks for a 'global figure', you should try not to say, 'Mickey Mouse'.

Grazing

For about a thousand years, to 'graze' was to be a sheep or a cow munching on pasture. Nowadays, we are all at it.

The word is Old English, taken from the word for grass, and used primarily for the eating habits of cattle, right up to the 1970s. 'Graze' also means to scrape the skin, but that's usually considered a different word.

The Anglo-Saxons took cattle too seriously to risk jokes, but by the eighteenth century, the verb 'to graze' was being humorously applied to people. One Lady Granville observed in a letter of 1824 that 'Mr Drummond does no harm grazing at the bottom of the table.'

This approaches our current sense, but you can be sure that Mr Drummond was sitting down and eating a proper meal rather than walking around with a packet of Cheesy Wotsits and a can of Tango.

Today, 'to graze' is to eat informally, or on the move. It comes in two distinct flavours. The first, recorded as early as 1978, refers simply to the modern practice of intermittent snacking. The second, first recorded in a 1979 *Daily Telegraph* report from America, means picking up and eating items of food while wandering through a supermarket without necessarily paying for them.

Like a hungry sheep, or a junk-munching shopper, language rarely stays still. The way we consume food, restlessly, without great attention, is increasingly the way we consume everything. So 'to graze' has come to mean 'to sample experiences haphazardly'.

So it is that, remote control in hand, we 'graze' the television channels. Or we 'graze' through the glossy magazines at the dentist's, or through the treasures of foreign lands. Consider this, from an article about the French Riviera: 'Cultural tourists can potter to Hauts-de-Cagnes and Cannes to graze on Picasso, Bonnard and Giacometti.' We are all ruminants now.

Grief

'Grief' is a devastating sense of loss, usually brought about by death. On the other hand, it's also a slight annoyance, brought about by domestic circumstances.

'I don't need this grief,' mutters the suburban Ulysses, failing to find a washer in B&Q and certain that Penelope, his 'trouble and strife', will give him 'grief' if he comes home without it. 'Grief', in other words, is what used to be called 'aggro' before that word, redolent of the skinhead era, wandered off to the slang museum.

'Grief', though, is a noble, dignified term, synonymous with bereavement. How did it end up in the mouths of television villains, chirpy Cockneys and wide-persons generally? It's a complicated story.

The ultimate source of 'grief' is the Latin *gravis*, meaning 'heavy'. From its first appearance in the thirteenth century, 'grief' applied to all manner of bad experiences and feelings: suffering, hardship; personal injury or offence; anger and displeasure. Rather like our slang use, but with a rather more serious level of 'aggro' (see the Book of Job for details).

It was only in the nineteenth century that 'grief' began to be reserved for the pain of loss, particularly bereavement. Theoretically, the earlier meanings are obsolete, but most of them seem in rude health, particularly in London. Did they survive in dialect, only to be reintroduced to standard English through *Minder*, *EastEnders*, and other examples of television anthropology?

More likely, the modern 'grief' grew out of 'come to grief', a nineteenth-century phrase meaning to meet with misfortune, usually by falling off a horse. Later 'grief' was used elliptically, to mean the misfortune itself. As the *Sportsman* reported, describing some racecourse incident of 1891: 'The flag had scarcely fallen than the grief commenced.'

The idiom is close to our own, except that in nineteenth-century sport any such 'grief' was likely to have been accidental.

Gross

Gross

'That's really gross,' you hear, or, more economically, 'Gross!' The accompanying facial expression indicates what the word means: disgusting, but more so.

'Gross' is a recent import from the US, where it is a favourite among students, teenagers and Valley Girls, the strange Californian subcultural group responsible for such linguistic arcana as 'Grody to the max!' and 'Gag me with a spoon!'

It came to prominence in the early 1970s, as the American *Saturday Review* nicely observed: 'as used by teens, it runs the gamut of awfulness, from homework to something the cat contributed to the ecology'.

In origin, 'gross' just means big. It's from the Late Latin *grossus*, meaning thick, via the French *gros*. The word has been used in English since the fifteenth century for large objects, fat people and other things that 'stand out', both physically and figuratively.

This is particularly true of vices: for four hundred years the adjective has been coupled with such nouns as 'ignorance', 'stupidity' and 'incompetence'. In other words, 'gross' not only means big, but big in a bad way.

And it gets worse. The word also meant 'coarse', because 'coarse' things are thick and have big lumps in them. 'Gross meat' was what the common people ate in the fifteenth and sixteenth centuries, and, since we are what we eat, they naturally became known as the 'gross people'.

The manners of these 'gross people' were, naturally, 'gross', which is to say crude, brutal and disgusting. Such luminaries as Shakespeare, Hobbes and Boswell used the word in precisely this way. Their 'gross' expressed a distaste more moral than physical, but they would certainly have grasped what the Valley Girls were going on about when they used the word.

'Gag me with a spoon!', however, might have given them pause.

Gutted

One of our architectural giants, a man at the very pinnacle of a noble profession, was interviewed about the way a competition had been organized. He wasn't happy. In fact, he said, he was 'gutted'.

A few years ago, this ugly expression was largely restricted to the occupational dialect of the professional footballer. Now it is soaring up the social scale. How long before we are solemnly informed that Her Majesty the Queen is 'gutted' about some patriotic setback or natural disaster?

There is no doubt about the word's meaning: deeply disappointed, devastated, shattered. But what does that have to do with being cut open and eviscerated like a fish?

For at least one thousand years, the 'guts' have been the innards, the contents of the intestinal cavity in man and beasts. In our own century, the word has also come to mean courage and strength of character. Since the 1960s, we have also discovered that a 'gut reaction' is a strong emotional response.

One thing that has remained consistent since the sixteenth century is that the 'guts' are the place where grief (q.v.) is felt. As Sir Philip Sidney put it in 1580, 'My eyes, my guts, yea my soule, griefe dost wast[e].'

In the school playgrounds of the 1960s, you were 'gutted' when someone punched you in the stomach and winded you. That may be what the modern 'gutted' is all about: a pain in the guts, albeit one more emotional than literal.

Our 'gutted' is, according to the experts, a prison use, although they are not normally seen as centres for the study of Elizabethan literature. But if it started there, it was soon more commonly heard from professional sportsmen, not to mention punters, litigants and the police. No High Court judges yet, but it's only a matter of time.

Holistic

Everyone is in favour of a 'holistic' approach, but almost no one can say what it means.

It's a label that has been applied to everyone from Dame Barbara Cartland to Jah Wobble and to everything from management to loving your inner child.

Naturally, the Prince of Wales was an early enthusiast. In successive sentences in a single interview, he once managed to call for 'holistic' approaches to architecture, agriculture and medicine. A useful word, then, especially for those with a duty to be vague.

'Holism' was invented in 1926 by Jan Smuts, barrister, soldier, statesman and part-time philosopher. Between two terms as Prime Minister of South Africa, he wrote *Holism and Evolution*, which claimed that nature tends to create wholes which are greater than the sum of their parts.

This may have been wishful thinking, since it mirrored his own political objectives: he was involved in creating the Union of South Africa, the League of Nations, the British Commonwealth and, later, the United Nations.

Smuts based his word on the Greek *holos*, meaning 'whole' or 'entire'. 'Holism' kicked around the world of philosophy for decades before being rediscovered in medical schools in the 1960s. They used it for a therapeutic approach that attempts to treat the whole person, rather than just the disease, which is why conscientious doctors sometimes ask 'Anything else?' before handing over your prescription.

'Alternative' and 'complementary' therapists borrowed the expression, as did other experts claiming, however rashly, to know 'the whole you' and to see 'the big picture'.

These days, you can adopt 'holistic management', visit a 'holistic priest', and take 'holistic financial advice' or a 'holistic massage'. You can even go 'holistic shopping', a discipline that requires you to ponder the fate of the earth's resources even as you are shovelling them into your trolley. As Jerry Lee Lewis might have said, there's a whole lot of 'holism' going on.

Icon

'Anyone of icon status, like me,' said Sandie Shaw, the self-effacing former pop star, 'realises that there has to be an interplay of deep unconscious fantasy between you and your audience . . .'

It's not much of an explanation, but it's at least as helpful as the traditional definition. These days, an 'icon' is rarely a work of religious art. More often it's someone famous – an ancient singer, perhaps – or a 'classic' object such as a chrome-plated toaster. But all 'icons' are the object of worship.

'Icon' is an Anglicized version of the Greek *eikon*, meaning 'likeness'. It appeared in English in the 1570s, meaning picture or illustration, with no religious implications. It has recently been revived in this sense to describe the helpful little pictures on a computer screen.

In the nineteenth century, however, it became the standard word for the devotional art of the Russian Orthodox Church. These 'icons' were considered sacred in themselves, and thus a focus for worship.

Our current meaning emerged in the 1980s, when dead or forgotten singers and actresses began to be written about on the grounds that they were 'gay icons'. In other words, gay people *worshipped* them.

Later, this approach was broadened, giving us 'pop icons', 'cultural icons', 'design icons' and more. Earlier in the century, the word 'icon' had become part of the impenetrable jargon of semiotics. In the 1980s, it emerged, bandied about by a new generation of writers, most of whom just liked the sound of it.

The simple 'icon', with no qualification, was most often applied to the singer Madonna. The first hundred or so writers to do this probably enjoyed the sacrilegious irony: the rest didn't even notice.

More recently, 'icon' has proven a usefully neutral term for Princess Diana, undeniably an object of veneration in life and death. Sandie Shaw, however, may be kidding herself.

Inappropriate

When children at a London junior school were sent home with a note warning that there had been 'inappropriate sex games' in the playground, parents were suspicious. 'I suppose appropriate sex games would have been all right?' snarled one.

It doesn't work like that. 'Inappropriate' is not simply the opposite of 'appropriate': it has a life of its own. In official practice, to call behaviour 'inappropriate' is to disapprove, without appearing to moralize.

Those in authority in public life know that eating people is wrong. But such 'judgemental' language can offend. Better to say that cannibalism is 'inappropriate', leaving open the possibility that it might be all right somewhere else, or in different circumstances.

There is now a thriving industry devoted to the production of guides to 'inappropriate behaviour', especially in America. In 1995, an unfortunate nurse in Spokane, Washington, made history, of a kind, when she was formally reprimanded for 'inappropriate handling of a human heart'. It had been donated for transplant, but she dropped it, then dumped it in a waste bin.

But 'inappropriate' is used particularly for minor sexual misdemeanours in office and institutional life, where things are more than embarrassing but less than criminal. Hence the goings-on in the playground.

'Inappropriate' and 'appropriate' both come from the Latin *proprius*, an adjective meaning 'one's own'. If something is 'appropriate' to someone it literally 'belongs to' them. But *proprius*, like 'appropriate', also means 'fit' or 'suitable'.

'Inappropriate' only arrived in the nineteenth century. Very quickly it acquired moral overtones: in *Dombey and Son*, published in 1848, someone sings an 'inappropriate air' at a grave occasion. It didn't 'belong' there, and that made it improper.

Indeed, to understand the modern non-judgemental 'inappropriate', we could hardly do better than replace it with that nineteenth-century formula: 'failing to observe the proprieties'. Victorian values, they call them.

Industrial

The word 'industrial' has found a new lease of life as the raw material for jokes. Female television presenters are said to wear 'industrial-strength' mascara. Scathing reviews of fashionable restaurants refer to their 'industrial ambience'. People breaking a nail on the photocopier are said to have acquired an 'industrial injury'.

Industry itself, meanwhile, prefers to talk about 'providing a service' rather than admit to making anything.

The word, like the thing itself, has had a rapid rise and fall. 'Industry', meaning 'diligence' and 'hard work', has been in English since the fifteenth century, as a translation of the Latin *industria*. But it is only in the last two hundred years that it has come to mean a society's manufacturing or wealth-creating activity. Adam Smith seems to have coined it in *Inquiry into the Nature and Causes of the Wealth of Nations*, of 1776, when he wrote about 'the funds intended for the maintenance of industry'.

In 1843, Carlyle spoke about 'the Leaders of Industry'. A year later Disraeli talked about 'our national industries' and the word had well and truly arrived. 'Industrial' arrived at about the same time, but was viewed by some as an alien adaptation of the French *industriel*. John Stuart Mill was not prejudiced, however, and in 1848 coined the expression 'industrial revolution' to describe what he saw around him.

Thereafter, compound nouns were rapidly churned out in vast quantities to meet every need: 'industrial soaps', 'industrial diseases', 'industrial disputes', 'industrial workers'. All now seem redolent of history.

In post-industrial Britain, the word 'industrial' tends to be used only with an ironic smirk, in the way you might wear a hammer and sickle on your Armani suit or keep a railwayman's lamp on the mantle of your Islington 'artisan's dwelling'.

There are no ironies, however, in the nation's 'industrial museums', where former coal miners are employed, pretending to dig coal for the benefit of incredulous schoolchildren.

Ish

Ish

It is lunchtime in the office. 'Are you hungry at all?' asks Jim. 'Ish,' replies Susie, keeping her options open: 'Are you going now?' 'Ish,' responds Jim. And so on.

What they are really saying is '-ish'. Susie is 'hungryish'. Jim is going 'nowish'. These days, though, 'Ish' can stand on its own, even where it has no grammatical business. 'Do you have time to see me this afternoon?' 'Ish.' Perhaps the best translation is 'maybe'.

You can't do this with those other adjective suffixes, '-able', '-ive', '-ful' and the rest. The '-ish' suffix is special, and very old, going back to the roots of the Germanic languages. In Old English it was used principally to describe the origins of people: Scottish, Netherlandish, Pictish and so on.

Less frequently it was used to mean 'resembling' or 'characteristic of', in, for example, *cildisc*, first recorded in about the year 1000, which we can just about recognize as 'childish'. Today, the '-ish' suffix tends to mean 'in a bad way', an implication that arrived in Tudor times. When we want to say 'like a child, in a good way', perhaps to applaud some *wunderkind* artist doing clever things with bodily fluids, we have to say 'childlike'.

When people use that free-standing 'Ish', however, they are adapting the use of the suffix to modify an adjective to mean 'nearly' or 'slightly'. This happened first with colours, with 'bluish' found first in the fourteenth century.

Since then, it has spread to other adjectives. Today, we can talk of a 'thirtyish chef in a plainish shirt and newish shoes', providing we have well-fitting dentures.

The ambiguities created by the various '-ish' suffixes were famously exploited by Jonathan Miller, in *Beyond The Fringe*, when he quipped, 'I'm not really a Jew; just Jew-ish.' Which, as grammatical jokes go, was a good one. Ish.

Issues

'I'm sensing that you have issues,' says Ricki Lake, queen of the American people-show, stepping between an unhappily married couple. As is traditional on these programmes, they look ready to tear one another's throats out.

'Issues', in contemporary American speech, are problems. One computer program may be described as having 'issues' with another, meaning they won't work together. A technician may be offered a job handling 'user issues', meaning the customers' difficulties.

Here the nuance is rare, but creeping in. On the *Today* programme, you sometimes hear people say, without further clarification, 'My members have all sorts of issues about this.' But most of us take the old-fashioned view that 'issues' are things to discuss and clarify rather than solid grievances. In America, however, the word has gone beyond the talking stage.

In origin, an 'issue' is the way out, or 'exit' from something: both words come from the Latin *exire*. Rivers and besieged townsfolk had issues, and so did human lives.

The word also meant outcome, or product: the 'issue' of a marriage was the children. Both magazines and banknotes have 'issues', because they 'go out' into circulation, although the magazines are quicker to the recycling plant.

The word 'issue' has always had a special significance in law, back to the fourteenth century. In ordinary speech, an 'issue' is a question awaiting resolution through discussion. But in legal language, the 'issue' is what is left after the talking, at the end of the process of presenting and testing evidence. It is the fundamental disagreement upon which judge or jury must decide.

The modern American version stems from that. In a society in which the aggrieved turn to either their lawyer or their gun, it is easy to see how a word meaning the 'point of disagreement' could come to mean 'problems', 'difficulties' or just plain 'trouble'.

It

Who remembers the 'It girls'? For a while, we were constantly told that this clique of vacuous Knightsbridge socialites had 'It'. But what was 'It'?

It's tempting to say 'too much money' and 'too little taste', but sadly no works of reference would support such an interpretation. *Tatler* magazine revived the eighty-year-old idea of 'It girls' when it said that Tara, Caprice, Tamara and a number of other walking soap-bubbles were the girls 'every female wants to be and every man wants to have'.

Hmm. The description was rather more appropriate for the first 'It girl', Clara Bow. Without benefit of dialogue, nudity or anything resembling a figure, Miss Bow shocked, scandalized and delighted the movie-going public throughout the 1920s.

Then, in 1927, she earned her *nom de guerre* by starring in *It*, the story of a girl who goes to ritzy events in flimsy clothes in search of a rich man. Odd that such a tale should have interested *Tatler*.

Both book and film were written by Elinor Glyn, now chiefly remembered for a piece of doggerel in which she starred alongside sin and a tiger skin. 'It' meant sex, and had for a very long time.

English people had been 'at it', in fact, since 1611. The Americans had another idea, however. To be 'It' in America, in the early years of our century, was to be 'the very thing' or 'the ultimate'.

Glyn slyly merged the two, as has *Tatler*. As she explains in the written titles at the start of the film: ' "It" is that quality possessed by some which draws all others with its magnetic force. With "It" you can draw all men, if you are a woman, and all women, if you are a man.

' "It" can be a quality of the mind, as well as a physical attraction,' she says. Apparently the regulations have been relaxed since then.

Key

You start your day with a few calls to 'key contacts', many of them 'key players' in 'key enterprises'. Later, a 'key worker' wants to discuss 'key issues' and 'key practices', but you disagree on 'key objectives'. No wonder you end your day 'keyed-up'.

'Key', only recently accepted as an adjective, means 'important', 'central' and 'crucial', which is very much its current status as a word. Odd, considering it started off as a tenth-century word for a piece of metal used for securing a lock.

The word has always had figurative uses. A 'key' unlocks an opportunity, or an area of knowledge, especially something mysterious. Thus you might say that 'plain-speaking is the key to dealing with the opposite sex'. You'd be wrong, but you might say it.

But today's 'key words' have a different source. They reflect the use of 'key' to mean a vital piece that holds things together: most obviously, the 'keystone' in an arch.

This seventeenth-century formation led, eventually, to all sorts of analogous words for important people and things. In 1916, the The Economist wrote nervously of something being a ' "key" industry', the inverted commas betraying its reluctance. But 'key witness', 'key figure' and 'key factor' followed, and the inverted commas fell away.

'Keyed-up', meanwhile, depends upon a different analogy, this time from music. A set of related musical notes is called a 'key' because that is a translation of the Latin *clavis*, the term used by the medieval monk who first taught people to sing from music rather than memory.

A person who is 'keyed-up' is someone who has been wound up to a higher pitch than perhaps they should be. 'Key personnel' in industry should be aware that this is a dangerous practice that can easily cause something – or someone – to snap.

Kit

Twice in one memorable evening, television viewers had the pleasure of hearing the actress Helen Mirren talking about 'getting my kit off'.

The first time she was in character, albeit one sending up her own racy reputation. The second time was in an advert for an airline, which apparently provides sufficient room for her to disrobe in comfort.

To 'get your kit off' is a typically British idiom, calculated to de-eroticize undressing, to turn sex into something hearty, like sport. Sport is the source of the expression, 'football kit' being boots, shirt, shorts and socks.

The word started appearing in a salacious context in the late 1980s. A young man would flick idly through a magazine, pausing at a picture of an attractive woman and murmuring, 'Get your kit off . . .' It seemed terribly witty at the time. Soon everyone (everyone male, that is) was saying it.

But endless repetition by the beer 'n' fags 'n' birds brigade, from the *Men Behaving Badly* to Chris Evans to *FHM* magazine, has not improved the joke. The same men also use the word to mean 'equipment' or 'hardware'. 'That's a beautiful piece of kit,' they might say, looking at someone's motorcycle, surround-sound digital television or high-performance all-weather anorak.

In its fourteenth-century origins, a 'kit' was a wooden tub or box. Later, it was a basket used for packing fish. Nothing very sexy there. In the eighteenth century, though, it was soldiers' slang for the equipment they carried in their knapsacks and the clothes they wore. Later, equipment of all sorts became 'kit'. So, too, did uniform, including the uniform worn by people in football teams.

Interestingly, there was a further development. 'The whole kit' was, apparently, a nineteenth-century term for the male genitals. In current circumstances, it is perhaps just as well that 'tackle', an angling term, has taken over this role.

Labour

How will history view 'New Labour'? As a marketing triumph like the 'New Seekers'? Or a disaster like 'New Coke'?

You can see where it came from. 'Labour' is such an old word for such a 'cool', 'with-it' party. It goes back, oh, to the beginning of the century, when the members of the Labour Representation Committee were bearded men who talked about socialism.

Actually, it goes back much further than that, to the Latin *labor*, which meant work, in its least attractive aspects: toil, exertion, hardship, distress. The Germanic 'work' had had all the positive connotations: 'labour', which arrived via French, is just unremitting slog. No one, for instance, ever went on a march demanding 'the right to labour'.

Its first appearance in English was at the beginning of the fourteenth century, in the *Cursor Mundi*, a slightly premature history of everything. The poem promises that both *Labur* and *Soru* (sorrow) will be abolished with the Second Coming: more recent writers have preferred the expression 'after the revolution'.

In Adam Smith's 1776 *Inquiry into the Nature and Causes of the Wealth of Nations*, 'labour' was used for the first time in its modern economic sense, to mean the body of work done within a community or society. From this stemmed the idea of 'labour' as 'those who do the work'. Hence the 'Labour Party', established in 1906 and now dismissed as 'Old Labour' by the smirking revisionists in the Millbank Tower.

'Labour' has another vital meaning, at least for 50 per cent of the human race, which is 'childbirth'. Again, the word's associations are with the pain rather than with the glory. Consequently, midwives are tending towards less frightening euphemisms. The 'labour ward', for instance, is now usually the 'delivery suite'.

The process itself, however, is still called 'labour'. You can only dress things up so far, as Tony Blair and his friends will discover.

Lad

Anyone who considers the *Oxford English Dictionary* a dull book has obviously never read the etymological notes on the word 'lad'.

The suggestion that 'lad' relates to *juggelaudi*, the Gothic word for 'young men' is 'quite inadmissible', apparently. Furthermore, the idea that it comes from Celtic roots (the Welsh *llodes* or the Irish *lath*) is 'worthless'. Talk about sticking the boot in: the 'lads' at Millwall would be proud.

Whatever its derivation (the *OED* suggests, rather drearily, that a 'ladde' was someone who was 'led') the word has not always been a term of affection. It began as a word for a servant or low person. In the York Mystery Plays of *c*.1440 it is an insult aimed at Jesus by those who want him crucified.

By the middle of the following century, however, it had become an indulgent expression for a boy or young man (it is what Falstaff often calls Prince Hal) and so it often remains. There's a poetic, sentimental strain in it too, starting in Elizabethan pastoral, where it meant a young shepherd, and carrying through as far as A. E. Housman's 1896 *A Shropshire Lad*.

For much of our century, though, to be 'a lad' or 'a bit of a lad' has been to be a slightly raffish adult. To quote *Seeds of Hate*, an amusingly prescient 1959 crime novel by one Harry Carmichael: 'Bit of a lad is Mr Alan Clark . . . running round fancy-free for years.'

Hence the pseudo-sociological 'lads', or sometimes 'new lads', of recent years. Endlessly analysed by commentators and courted by advertisers, these are men of indeterminate age who fancy themselves as smoking, drinking, football-supporting, skirt-chasing rebels against the milk-and-water 'new man' ethos of recent years. You can't move for them down at the crèche.

Larging it

'Do anything nice last night?' asks the hairdresser, in one of those riveting fly-on-the-wall documentaries about people getting their hair cut. 'Yes,' says the client, 'I was larging it.' And they laugh.

Once 'larging it' or 'giving it large' was a male thing, promoted in the alleged men's magazines. It meant drinking, smoking, shouting, swearing and generally behaving in ways incompatible with membership of a public library. But now women are doing it too: this must be what they mean by 'girl power'.

But why 'larging it'? There was once a verb 'to large'. If you were in a boat you could say, 'I'm going to large the shore.' But there is little in this that reflects the leisure pursuits of the young and stupid.

Luckily, the adjective 'large' is large, and contains multitudes. It arrived in the twelfth century, a borrowing of the French *large*, itself derived from the Latin *larga*, meaning abundant. In early English the word meant first generous, or open-handed, then ample or roomy, and finally broad, only arriving at the principal modern definition, big, in the sixteenth century.

But it also meant lax or free. If a judge was 'large' in the seventeenth century, it didn't mean his Weight Watchers membership had lapsed, it meant he was soft. Even today, to be 'at large' is to be at liberty.

Could it be that those 'larging it' are actually enjoying themselves in the desperate manner of fugitives expecting imminent recapture and retribution? Wishful thinking, probably.

Some say the new usage came from Black American speech, noting its appearance in the language of US adolescents. But we may not have to look that far. In nineteenth-century slang, 'large' meant 'excessively'. You might 'dress large' (showily), 'go large' (noisily) or 'talk large' (boastfully).

Just the kind of evening, in fact, to tell your hairdresser – and several million television viewers – all about.

Legacy

A 'legacy' is generally seen as a good thing, whether it's a thriving country estate or an exquisite die-cast model of Dr Who's *Tardis*.

Since Tudor times, the word has meant money or an object left in a will: a bequest. More recently, from the eighteenth century or so, it has come to mean anything, concrete or abstract, that is handed down to a successor, even by someone who is still alive.

For instance, a football manager who is sacked (and they all are) is said to leave a 'legacy'. This tends to mean eleven players and a certain way of accepting defeat, rather than a nylon anorak and a bottle of Gaviscon.

When the word is used in this figurative way, it is perfectly possible to leave an 'awful legacy', particularly if you are the dictator of an artificially constructed Balkan state. But the same could be said if you owned a fish shop and ran away without first removing the stock.

Now, though, something has happened to 'legacy'. In the computer world, people have constructed new compounds, in which 'legacy' is almost an adjective: 'legacy data', 'legacy applications' and 'legacy systems'. They mean the technology an organization is using when the experts arrive with something new.

Since everything in computing is out of date as soon as it comes out of the shrink-wrap, the experts naturally consider these 'legacy' files, programs and machines to be less than useless. But they have to work with them, at first, since they tend to contain the essence of the client's business.

Frustration is inevitable. Thus the word 'legacy' is becoming tinged, for the first time, with contempt. So useful is the expression, however, that it seems only a matter of time before similar experts arrive to tell us that our real problem is 'legacy practices' and 'legacy personnel'. Then we really will be in trouble.

To liaise

The French gave us the word 'liaison'. But the verb 'to liaise', which it spawned, is all our own.

In French, *une liaison* (from the Latin *ligation*, a noun meaning 'the act of binding') covers all manner of unions, connections, acquaintanceships and intimacies. But in English it has usually been linked to those things for which the French have a reputation, however undeserved.

Thus, in the seventeenth and eighteenth centuries, it meant a thickening for sauces, made from eggs. Then, following the 1782 publication of *Les liaisons dangereuses*, it was a fashionable term for a sexual adventure, first used in English by Byron.

In World War I, our boys encountered French *liaison* officers, charged with organizing communication between the Allied Forces, and adopted the term. No equivalent verb existed, so we invented one. Lord Fisher, First Sea Lord, is the first person recorded as using it, in 1916: 'I want a soldier to keep in touch with the Navy and so "liaise" or exchange inventions which may be suitable.'

It was still remarkable in 1941, when an American journal praised the 'grammatical economy' of a Home Guard leaflet in which two groups were told to 'liaise' with one another, presumably so they didn't both shout 'Don't panic!' at once. After demobilization, such vocabulary found its way into civilian life.

Today, 'liaison' retains an element of *double-entendre*, perhaps because of its suspiciously 'Continental' sound, not to mention our familiarity with *Dangerous Liaisons*, the film of the translation of the title of the play of the book.

To 'liaise', however, has magically regained its linguistic virginity. 'I'll liaise with you later, if I may, June,' says the personnel director, and no one turns a hair. Whereas if he had said, 'I'll come round and sort you out later', June would have been consulting her pamphlet on sexual harassment quicker than you can say Choderlos de Laclos.

Liberal

They may call themselves the 'Liberal Democrats', but to most people they'll always be the 'Liberals'. After all, call yourself a 'Democrat' and you're teaming up with the likes of George Wallace and Erich Honeker.

The adjective 'liberal' is a fourteenth-century adaptation of the Latin *liberalis*, which means 'pertaining to a free man', and by extension 'gentlemanly', 'well-bred' and 'generous'.

In late medieval England, a gentleman would thus have received a 'liberal education' and been required to provide 'liberal' hospitality. Later, though, the word acquired derogatory nuances. After 'liberal' indulgence in food and drink, Elizabethan gentlemen were inclined to become 'liberal' in their speech and behaviour.

In *Othello*, for instance, Desdemona calls Iago a 'liberal counsellor', and she doesn't mean he calls round to ask her views on cracked pavements.

In the enlightened eighteenth and nineteenth centuries, being 'liberal' was once again praiseworthy: it meant forward-looking and broad-minded, especially in matters of religion. On the Continent, however, those calling themselves 'liberals' were a frightening bunch: they were also called 'democrats', by the way.

So when opponents of nineteenth-century reform wanted to tarnish the more radical of the Whigs, they called them 'Liberales' and 'Liberaux', using pseudo-French because the English 'liberal' retained too many good connotations.

The radicals, however, happily adopted the epithet. Hence the Liberal Party, still with us, in both Liberal-Democrat and undiluted Liberal flavours, despite regular predictions of its demise.

Unlike, say, 'Social Democrat', which sounds Germanic and sinister to anyone with a smattering of history, 'Liberal' continues to have an appealing resonance, at least in Britain: in the US it seems to be a swear word.

It is likely to do so as long as head teachers are prepared to take a 'liberal attitude' to minor infractions, free gifts are 'liberally distributed' and the sexually active are described as 'liberal with their favours'.

Loft

Loft

It was in the late 1970s that word of the vibrant New York 'loft' scene first reached the ears of incredulous Britons.

Apparently, artists were living and working in 'lofts', while avant-garde theatre groups and punk-rock bands performed around them. But how did they manage to avoid tripping over the old gardening clothes, the bundles of magazines and the abandoned model railway layouts? And why didn't they bump their heads on the roof?

It soon became clear that this was a word just different enough on opposite sides of the Atlantic to cause serious confusion. To the Americans it meant an upper floor in an industrial building. To us it was a place to keep tennis rackets with no strings.

This confusion has ancient roots. In Old English, and before that in the Norse of the Vikings, *loft* meant 'air' and 'sky', which is why tall people (not to mention short people) are called 'Lofty'. But it also meant 'upper room'.

But what kind of upper room? In the King James Bible of 1611, 'loft' appears twice. In the First Book of Kings it means an upstairs bedroom. Then, in the Acts of the Apostles, the story is told of a young man who nodded off while listening to St Paul and 'fell down from the third loft, and was taken up dead'.

Both modern meanings are here. The upstairs bedroom became, on this side of the Atlantic, an upper room where you store things (pigeons, for instance, or hay). The second meaning, a floor or storey, was adopted in America to mean the upper parts of factories and warehouses.

Thanks to the opportunism of estate agents, the bare upper floors of redundant British industrial buildings are now habitually advertised as 'lofts'. That vibrant New York lifestyle, however, continues to prove elusive.

Logistics

Management tip: if you can't change your business, change its name. This may be why so many long-distance lorry operators now claim to be in the business of 'logistics'.

Whereas 'haulage' and 'transport' suggest grease-stained truckers crawling up and down the M1 in a cloud of diesel, the word 'logistics' sounds cerebral, hi-tech – and clean. But it has these associations on false pretences.

'Logistic' appeared in the seventeenth century, derived from *logos*, the Greek for 'word' or 'reason'. It meant 'logical'. Later it was revived as the name for a type of mathematical logic. The plural, 'logistics', was used for various types of arithmetic, notably the sexagesimal calculations used in astronomy.

Tempting though it is to imagine Britain's lorry-drivers navigating by the stars, that would be a mistake. Their 'logistics' comes instead from the French *logistique*, a term invented by Baron de Jomini, author of *Summary of the Art of War*, in the nineteenth century. It meant the business of supplying your troops with not only *logis*, or lodgings, but food, boots, uniforms and the rest.

The term was adopted by the American military from the Civil War onwards. We caught up in 1993, when various Army transport organizations were reconstituted as, idiosyncratically, the Royal Logistic Corps.

'Logistics' first escaped from military life in the period of the Vietnam War: in her 1963 diary, Lady Bird Johnson, wife of the US President, frets about the 'logistics' of a visit from the German Chancellor to their Texas ranch. If Ludwig Erhard ate as much as some recent incumbents, you can imagine the problem.

In 1985, with Vietnam in the past, it seems to have been renewed military glamour that encouraged America's National Council of Physical Distribution Management to change its name to The Council of Logistics Management.

Since then, trucks with 'logistics' on the side have been common there, and now, inevitably, they're common here.

Lunch

Lunch

A change of preposition can make a world of difference. 'Out to lunch': insane, crazy, eccentric. 'Out at lunch': not in the office.

For long periods in the 1980s, no one was in the office. They were 'at lunch'. The excuse was that 'lunch' was really a meeting, with food: there was 'working lunch', 'power lunch' and, less acceptably, 'liquid lunch'.

Then came 'Lunch is for wimps!', bellowed by Michael Douglas in *Wall Street*, and suddenly the men in red braces started ordering in, leaving plenty of table space for 'the ladies who lunch'.

It was just a phase. New Britain is very much 'on for lunch', especially if you like polenta.

Which came first, 'lunch' or 'luncheon'? Actually, they arrived together at the end of the sixteenth century, derived from the Spanish *lonja*, meaning a slice of ham. They meant a hunk of bread or cheese or cold meat.

What better for a mid-morning snack, still the principal sense of 'lunch' for the non-lunching classes, who tend to call their midday meal 'dinner'. Such snacks are often carried to work in a 'lunch box', a word otherwise reserved for the genitalia of certain sports stars.

The Victorians ate 'luncheon' at midday, scorning 'lunch' as vulgar. But today 'luncheon' survives only as a formal event, usually featuring the Lord Mayor, in 'luncheon vouchers', and as 'luncheon meat', a slippery pink substance designed to accompany sliced white bread.

While everyone wants 'lunch', no one wants to be it. In the lexicon of Australian surfing, 'lunch' is what you become if you fall off: shark-food, in other words. The idea of forming a snack for someone more aggressive is persistent. American students called such a person 'lunch', or 'lunchy', which may be one source of 'out to lunch'.

But, fundamentally, a person who is 'out to lunch' is somewhere else – and you're not invited.

Lush

What do people mean when they say something they like is 'lush'? It's easier to say what they don't mean.

They don't mean 'lush' meaning 'luxuriant' and applied to grass, colours, orchestration and the prose style of Mr A. A. Gill. Nor do they mean 'lush' meaning a drinker, heard first in Britain in 1790.

Most likely, the current, youthful 'lush' is a shortened form of 'luscious'. But not necessarily. It has a history of its own. In the nineteenth century, it was Eton slang for 'dainty'. In World War I, soldiers used it of female pulchritude, referring to 'a lush bint'. In the 1960s, the expression was 'a lush bird': this was, you understand, Before Feminism.

To the schoolchildren of that era, however, both 'lush' and 'luscious' meant simply 'desirable' and applied to anything from a model of James Bond's Aston Martin – with ejector seat – to the whey-faced stars of *Top of the Pops*. Now, while the objects of desire have changed, the word lives on.

'Luscious' itself may have started as a fifteenth-century variation on 'licious', a shortened form of 'delicious'. 'Lush' was around at the same time, derived from French and meaning soft, slack or feeble.

Shakespeare somehow picked it up and used it quite erroneously in *The Tempest* ('How lush and lusty the grass looks'). But it was his version that came to dominate in the 'poetic' nature writing of the nineteenth century and later. It appears in Keats, Shelley, Tennyson and most famously in William Boot's 'Lush Places'.

Both 'luscious', in the seventeenth century, and 'lush', in the nineteenth, acquired sexual connotations. From there to the Tommies' 'lush bint' is no distance at all. But then the sex faded, leaving only desire.

For example, consider 'The Fat Slags' in the teenage comic *Viz*. 'I love your ski pants,' says one. '*Tray* nice, aren't they?' '£12.99,' says the other. 'You want to get some. You'll look lush.'

Mad

In one of those periods when half the country's teenagers seemed to be organizing their own crime waves, one was asked what he thought about his town. 'It's cush,' he said. 'Peterlee is sorted. It's mad because you can do what you want.'

Amongst this welter of demotic ('cush' = cushy; 'sorted' = all right) you might have missed that 'mad'. He didn't mean Peterlee was insane because it let him do what he wanted (although, clearly, it was), nor that the town was angry about it (ditto). What he meant was that the town was 'great' or 'brilliant'.

'Mad' is a common term of approbation, but it implies something is 'out of control'. There would seem to be a connection with drugs. Not for nothing was Manchester nicknamed 'Madchester' at the start of the E-crazed 1990s. The same cultural hotspot gave us 'mad for it', a phrase and philosophy dedicatedly embraced by Liam Gallagher of Oasis.

'Mad' has always implied a departure from reality, usually through insanity. It appeared in its current form in the fourteenth century. Previously an Old English equivalent, *gemæded*, had been used. The word's origins are in an Indo-Germanic verb meaning 'to change'.

The other meanings – foolish, wildly enthusiastic, uncontrollably angry – are just as old, and all imply serious loss of grip. Only more recently has 'mad' come to mean 'slightly annoyed'. People blame the Americans, but they're wrong. It's even found in Trollope.

As a clinical term, 'mad' is frowned upon because of its note of contempt. Nonetheless, it can be used in an affectionate, indulgent way, implying only a mild, amusing eccentricity. We have all met people who announce, like Rik in *The Young Ones*, 'I'm mad, I am.' They aren't.

Interestingly, just like 'gay' and 'Black', 'mad' is being 'reclaimed' by those it was once used against. One Internet discussion area for ex-psychiatric patients, for instance, is proud to call itself 'Madness'.

Mall

Mall

British town centres used to have 'precincts': paved areas featuring shops, a flower bed and a bench. Now, we have the 'mall', an out-of-town shopping paradise with air-conditioning and bored security guards.

Originally, a 'mall' was a mallet, from the Latin *malleus*, meaning hammer. Mallets were used in the game known as *pallamaglia* (or 'mallet-ball') in Italy and *palle-maille* in France. We called it 'pall-mall' or just 'mall'.

This seventeenth-century sporting sensation involved whacking a boxwood ball towards an iron ring suspended high above the ground. It was a kind of aerial golf. To keep casualties to a minimum, a long alley bordered by trees was required, and this came to be called a 'mall'. One, in St James's Park, London, was so important that it became 'The Mall' (which rhymes with 'pal'). Pall Mall was another.

Later, when it was safe, these leafy corridors became places for the fashionable to promenade. And that elegant practice was consciously evoked by the town planners of the 1960s, who applied the word 'mall', without apparent irony, to the kind of bleak pedestrian wind tunnels that look so good in architectural drawings.

Today's 'mall' (which rhymes with 'ball') is an American-style enclosed shopping centre, including cinemas, fast-food joints and all the other paraphernalia of 'mall culture'.

And what is 'mall culture'? In a 1985 *Peanuts* strip, Peppermint Patty explained that she was going 'over to the shopping mall. We're "mallies". We like to hang around with the other mallies.'

That is about as interesting as 'malling' gets, but it doesn't stop the teenage 'mall-rats' (today's preferred term) gathering in such numbers as to create the odd 'mall-jam', usually involving drinking, shoplifting, fighting and, most worryingly, not buying anything.

It could be worse, however. They could be smashing wooden balls through the air.

-merchant

When politicians attacked 'squeegee-merchants', everyone knew what they meant. But why 'squeegee-*merchant*'? Surely such a person ought to *sell* you a strip of gritty rubber on the end of a stick rather than scraping one across your windscreen and demanding money for the privilege?

A 'merchant' has been someone who buys and sells since the word arrived in English, around 1300. Originally, it meant any kind of trader, including shopkeepers. It still does in the north, Scotland and the US, where everything from the corner kiosk to K-Mart is proud to be a 'merchant'.

In the rest of Britain, however, 'merchant' increasingly meant those trading in large quantities or with foreign countries. The King James Bible, for instance, tells us that 'the virtuous woman . . . is like the merchant's ships; she bringeth her food from afar'. How true, especially in these days of out-of-town shopping.

But none of this explains 'squeegee-merchant'. Far from being new, however, that expression oddly reflects the banter of the mid-sixteenth century, when a 'merchant' was simply a 'fellow' or a 'bloke'. In the eighteenth century, a 'caper-merchant' was a dancing master. The similarity with 'squeegee-merchant' is obvious, but by the end of that century the expression had disappeared.

The revival began a century ago. A theatre review of 1886 referred to a comedian as the 'low-comedy merchant', possibly because contemporary actors had begun referring to their place of work as 'the shop', and themselves as the 'merchants'. This new idiom was taken up. By 1914 we had 'speed-merchant', then 'doom-merchant', and many more, making 'squeegee-merchant' inevitable.

Surprisingly, 'squeegee' is nothing new either. It has been known in yachting circles since the 1840s, when a strip of 'gutta-percha' on the end of a stick was referred to, for reasons unknown, as a 'squee gee'.

Mint

For a few seconds, the fashionable way for the young to express approval was to say 'Mint!' Here's the proof, a children's television presenter introducing an orgy of badly-drawn violence: 'There's a really mint cartoon coming up.'

It's not fashionable any more, but it'll probably come round again very soon. As it is, some will recall that the same adjective was the height of fashion once before.

In the early 1970s, it flourished, alongside flared trousers and platform shoes. Watching that lot come round again, only to disappear again, has been an oddly ageing experience, like thinking policemen look young or developing a taste for Radio Two.

Actually, 'mint' has existed as an adjective throughout the century, simply as a quicker way of saying 'in mint condition'. A 'mint' stamp – or a 'mint' copy of Chicory Tip's *Son of My Father*, for that matter – is one so perfect as to resemble a newly-minted coin. The 'mint' under discussion here is an extension of that to mean 'excellent' in a more general sense.

But 'mint' is an interesting word in its own right. It is said to have begun with the Roman goddess Juno. Her full title was Juno Moneta, with *moneta* meaning 'she who warns'. But Juno Moneta was also in charge of financial matters, and the Roman mint was inside her temple. *Moneta* thus became the word for both the mint and the coins it produced.

That single Latin word found its way into both Germanic and Romance languages. In the former it became 'mint', our normal word for money until the fifteenth century. In the latter, it became 'money', which arrived in English from French in the fourteenth century, leaving 'mint' to describe the place where money is coined.

Now all we need is for someone to revive the tank top.

Mission

Your 'mission', should you choose to accept it, is not to preach The Word, nor to help the poor, nor to go behind enemy lines armed only with a length of twine and a rolled-up newspaper.

Instead, as your 'mission statement' says, you are to 'put the customer first', to 'make quality job one', and to 'offer a one-stop-shop solution' to anyone who understands what that might mean.

This is not what W. S. Gilbert had in mind when he coined the expression 'a man with a mission' in *Patience*. He meant someone with a sense of purpose. But strictly speaking the impetus for a 'mission' must come from outside: as it invariably does for anyone landed with a 'mission statement'.

'Mission' comes from the Latin verb *mittere*, 'to send', and traditionally it was God, or someone close to God, who did the sending. The word came into English at the end of the sixteenth century, to describe the journeys undertaken by the Jesuits from Catholic Europe to Protestant England, where a warm welcome awaited them.

Later, 'mission' was used for trade and diplomatic journeys. The Americans, in our own century, started to use the word for military tasks. The space programme and *Star Trek* made it glamorous.

Since the 1980s, the word has been a favourite of the flip-chart folk now ruining (sorry, *running*) industry. Organizations are broken into 'units', each with its own 'mission'. The units battle it out, and before long you've got the modern BBC. Or something.

Alternatively, the whole organization shares a 'mission'. The 'mission statement' is thus the 'same hymn sheet' from which everyone 'sings', provided they don't throw up first.

But what started as a management device, to help an organization do a good job, has increasingly turned into a public relations device – to help it *say* it's doing a good job. Not the same thing at all.

Monster

Monster

'It was bad,' agreed the man on the radio, discussing the behaviour of some footballers on an aeroplane. 'But it wasn't monster bad.'

Is it possible to use the word 'monster' as an adverb, a synonym for 'very'? It is now. The speaker here, a sports agent called Eric Hall, has made the idiom his own. But that's not to say it won't catch on.

Previously the word was most especially associated with Nigel Kennedy, the violinist. 'Monster!', he would often exclaim, whether he meant 'excellent', 'all right', 'I do so like Jimi Hendrix' or 'Could we redo the *sul ponticello* passage after bar 142?'

'Monster' comes from the Latin *monstrum*. Derived from the verb *monere*, to warn, that meant something that was both unnatural and a bad omen. In English, from the fourteenth century, it meant something extraordinary but not necessarily bad. Chaucer talks of 'that marvellous monster Fortune', for instance, and that was even before the invention of the National Lottery.

At the same time, 'monster' was the standard word for an animal or person afflicted with a congenital deformity. Frightening fictional beasts, especially big ones, were another example. Since the sixteenth century 'monster' has also been used of people whose deformities are moral rather than physical: it remains a standby of the tabloids.

Strangely, these grisly associations have never prevented its use as a faintly jocular way of saying 'big'. The Victorians were fond of 'monster ships' and 'monster balloons'. Shops today have 'monster sales' and 'monster offers'.

Shakespeare uses a verb 'to monster', meaning to turn someone into a monster. Today's tabloid journalists speak of being sent to 'monster' people, which means crawling all over their lives to gather material calculated to make them look unattractive. The same word, and a not dissimilar idea.

To morph

'Anthea is slowly morphing into Cilla,' observed a television critic. Five years ago, few of us would have had a clue what he meant. Walking into Cilla? Falling? Gnawing her way?

The answer is 'changing'. Once the preserve of film and computer graphics technicians, the verb 'to morph' is now very familiar, at least to those of us who haven't spent the last few years in the Marianas Trench.

One reason for this is the continued success of the Mighty Morphin Power Rangers, the team of inappropriate role models who first occupied the nation's toyshops in the Christmas of 1994. How many people found themselves asking which of the overpriced plastic figurines was Mighty Morphin himself?

Only later did we discover that Morphin was really Morphin', and that 'morphing' was what they were all doing when they changed from dozy American schoolchildren to colour-coordinated masters of the martial arts.

The verb 'to morph' is a contraction of that tongue-twister 'to metamorphose', from the Greek *metamorphosis*, a transformation. Older readers will recall 'Morph', an animated Plasticine figure of the early 1970s whose fluid movements prefigured Wallace & Gromit. But modern 'morphing' had to wait until technology had advanced beyond a lump of modelling clay and a camera.

True 'morphing' is where one image in digital form is changed into another through a series of visible stages. This permits the creation not only of the mythical Anthilla – half Anthea, half Cilla – but many more creatures, possibly even more terrifying, in which the two are mixed in uneven proportions.

These days you can carry out these magical transformations on quite modest computer equipment, using software from Woolworth's. No wonder so many adverts now show men changing into animals, animals changing into objects and attractive young women changing into underwear.

Mufti

In my nightmare, I put on my suit and tie and went to a meeting, only to find everyone else in gardening clothes. But it wasn't a nightmare: it was a 'mufti day'.

A 'mufti day' is when office workers wear home clothes and, in gratitude, give money to a good cause. In this case, they were journalists, so the clothes had to be spectacularly scruffy for anyone to notice – and they were.

The event dates back to the 1970s, when schools introduced charitable 'wear what you want days' as a change from sponsored litter collection and fêtes worse than death. Later the event spread to corporate life, acquiring its new name.

American companies and their imitators sometimes have 'dress down Fridays' or 'casual days', but the expression 'mufti day' is unknown in the US, and so is the charitable angle. But 'mufti days' are found in Australia, New Zealand and the Far East.

The magazine of St Joseph's School, in Sarawak, Malaysia, has put forward the theory that the event was invented by 'General Mufti, who found that sagging morale in the British Army was boosted by the policy of allowing the men to wear civilian clothing instead of uniforms on certain days of the year'.

Certainly, 'mufti' is a military expression. It is first recorded in 1816, in *Grand Master* by 'Quiz', an adventure based on the imperial exploits of the British in India. The hero takes off his dingy 'mufti' and dons his 'red', a typically sporting gesture in an era when uniforms were designed to provide a good target.

A *mufti*, though, is a Muslim priest or Islamic judge. The word is Arabic, meaning 'one who makes a fatwa'. British officers thought their off-duty dressing gowns, smoking caps and slippers made them look rather like Eastern religious leaders.

And so they did, or at least those they'd seen in *Aladdin* and *Ali Baba*.

Naïve

The resident fop on one of the television decorating programmes was daubing stripes of red and green emulsion at right angles on a piece of wood. It was, he declared, a 'naïve tartan'.

A dangerous usage, you might think, especially if employed North of the Border: 'Love the skirt, man. Pity the tartan's so naïve.' But these days 'naïve' is rather sophisticated. Psychologists study 'naïve physics', the ways in which children try to explain the world. 'Naïve art' is highly prized. The philosophy of 'naïve realism' won the support of A. J. Ayer. And so on.

Nonetheless, 'naïve', in English, usually means uninformed, ignorant and clueless. It's a sad story: *naïf*, a simple, good-hearted French adjective, comes to Britain, is involved in a mysterious change of gender, and turns nasty.

Naïf is the masculine form, from the Latin *nativum*, meaning native. *Naïve* is the feminine form. In French, both mean simple, artless and natural.

'Naïf' came to Britain at the end of the sixteenth century, with 'naïve' following half a century later. Neither was pejorative. But in the dangerous nineteenth century, to be simple, artless and natural was plain foolish. 'Naïf' and 'naïve' soon became terms of abuse.

But there are exceptions. In the 1940s, people began to praise the vision of the odd 'naïf painter': not a tousle-haired dandy toting a five-litre can of Dulux, but an artist without formal training. 'Naïf' was technically correct – they were generally male – but they became 'naïve painters' and 'naïve artists' because that sounded better.

Psychological labs are full of 'naïve rats', not rodents who think they're in a holiday camp, but those who have never been the subject of an experiment. But the first 'naïve subjects' in psychology experiments, in the 1940s, were human.

In one wonderful 1960s experiment, 'marijuana naïve' volunteers were given a placebo, but still emerged convinced that they'd been tripping. Too much television decorating can have the same effect.

Nerd

'We are all nerds now,' suggests an article in a magazine. What an outrageous slur. If I could only sort out the right SMTP/POP3 settings to dial up my ISP, I'd fire off an angry e-mail.

As it happens, 'nerd' (sometimes 'nurd') has never had anything to do with computers, engineering or science, as such. It's a meaningless insult, traditionally used by the student in-crowd against the unfashionable. And doing difficult things with numbers, wires and apparatus has long been as unfashionable as it gets.

But while we were hanging around the bar being witty, those 'nerds' were busy inventing the modern world – and becoming its richest inhabitants.

Never mind. We can console ourselves with the knowledge that 'nurd' may well be no more than a euphemistic modification of 'turd'. Alternatively, it may have come from a 'Dr Seuss' rhyme of 1950: 'And then, just to show them, I'll sail to Ka-Troo, / And bring back an It-Kutch, a Preep and a Proo, / A Nerkle, a Nerd, and a Seersucker, too!'

'Nerd' (but not 'Proo', 'Preep' or 'Nerkle') seems to have started among surfers and hot-rodders in 1960s California and spread to the campuses. Intriguingly, though, a 1957 reference from the Glasgow *Sunday Mail* gets it absolutely right: 'Nerd – a square'.

There may be a connection with a dimly-remembered British expression of the 1950s and 1960s, 'nerk' or 'nurk', meaning a fool or objectionable person. This clung on into the 1970s, when it featured in Ronnie Barker's *Porridge*, set in the only prison in the world without swearing. 'Nerk' may have been a substitute for 'berk', a word then banned in the early evening on account of its shocking origins, too well-known to mention here.

Did 'nerk' become 'nerd'? It wouldn't be the first time a British invention was taken up and improved before sweeping the world. As any 'nerd' will tell you.

Niche

A young journalist was describing her magazine. 'You won't have heard of us,' she said. 'We're very niche.'

This is grammatically unorthodox – 'niche' is usually a noun – but the meaning is plain. We don't print very many copies, but that's because we prefer it that way: no, really, we do.

Remarkably, the use of 'niche' as business jargon is said to have a single origin. According to the *Oxford Dictionary of New Words*, it appeared in the 1963 hit, *The Role of the Entrepreneur in Social Change in Northern Norway*. And titles don't come more 'niche' than that.

In the 1980s, 'niche' became an important term in business. This was the decade that gave us 'niche marketing', 'niche players' and the unforgettable 'nichemanship', embodied by the likes of Tie Rack, Sock Shop and Knickerbox.

'Niche' is said to derive from *nicchio*, an Italian word meaning 'mussel-shell'. The first 'niche' in English, in 1611, was 'a hollow seat, or standing for a statue, made into a wall'. It is still used this way.

Then, in the eighteenth century, people began to find themselves a 'niche in life'. This was either a prominent position in which they would be recognized, or a dark hole in which they could lurk: the word also meant the home of a spider or beetle.

It is tempting to see in this our modern use, some 'niche' retailers having colonized the dingier corners of railway stations and shopping centres. But a 'niche' operation is really a business that pursues customers that bigger concerns let slip: those, for instance, who can't pass through a railway station without buying socks.

The business term is thus a borrowing from ecology: the 'niche' occupied by a species is the way it manages to survive among other animals, usually by eating some and being food for others.

How apt. As many 'niche' businesses have found, it really is a jungle out there.

On-message

In the past, an ambitious Labour MP would aim to be a 'good comrade', a 'party loyalist' or even, whisper it, a 'staunch socialist'. The current generation know that the thing to be is 'on-message'.

And as long as you don't go 'off-message', which is to say, develop independent attitudes, it doesn't appear to matter what else Labour MPs do, from sending their children to a selective school to walking around the House without underwear.

According to Erskine May, the oracle of parliamentary practice, a 'message' is a communication between Sovereign and Parliament, or between the two Houses. But New Labour's 'on-message' is not about that.

The word 'message' arrived in the fourteenth century, from French, when it tended to mean news or information of diplomatic or military importance. Then, from the sixteenth century, it was used particularly for communications from God. You can see how that connection might appeal to those currently wielding political power.

In the nineteenth and twentieth centuries, a 'message' came to mean the dominant or underlying meaning of something, for instance a book. But since the 1960s, people have been bluntly advising one another to 'get the message', meaning to accept some veiled instruction or threat. You can see how that, too, might appeal to politicians.

But a 'message' is not only something you receive and understand. It is also something you carry, without opening it, reading it or arguing about it. Does 'on-message' carry an echo of that? To be 'on-message', as MPs have learned, is to convey information from the leadership to the voters without subjecting it to any unauthorized scrutiny.

It is amusing to note that to send someone 'on message' originally meant to send them on an errand. Another indication, perhaps, of the high status in which Labour backbenchers are held, now that there are more than four hundred of them.

Out

From the era of Jane Austen to that of Barbara Cartland the only people to 'come out' were debutantes in search of husbands. How things have changed.

'Out', in the sense of 'openly homosexual', is a recent development for this most versatile of words, which boasts at least thirty adverbial meanings, including 'unconscious', 'unfashionable' and 'not batting'. As an adjective, for instance in the phrase 'out members of the Cabinet', it is newer still.

'Out' surfaced here in 1979, in the unlikely setting of the letters page of the *Radio Times*, not normally considered to be in the forefront of sexual liberation. 'If you publish this letter,' wrote a reader, 'I would be grateful if you would withhold my full name, because I am not yet fully "out".' How baffling that must have been to those searching for the time of *Sing Something Simple*.

To 'come out' was really to 'come out of the closet', an American expression of the late 1960s. The closet had long been the metaphorical refuge of the secret homosexual. Another first for Britain, apparently, the term having been heard in London as early as the 1940s. But 'closet' has now largely lost its sexual connotations. 'I'm a closet Catholic,' people say, meaning only that they don't shout about it.

More recently a transitive verb 'to out' has arrived, meaning to expose a person's homosexuality to public scrutiny. One odd feature of this is that even now it is often practised by other homosexuals. In 1990, however, the tycoon Malcolm Forbes was 'outed', and that gave the expression vast international publicity.

The same year, a provocatively-titled new magazine, *OutWeek*, arrived on the New York gay scene, making a special feature of 'outings'. Readers expecting details of charabanc trips to places of interest would, however, have been disappointed.

Package

Package

When you see a job advertisement offering '35K + package', you somehow know that it won't come covered in brown paper and tied up with string. The same goes for the 'package offered by ITV this Christmas', and the 'package represented by the Ford Focus'.

A 'package' in this sense is a collection of items, concrete or abstract, intended to entice. When advertising a job, offering a 'package' with the 35K – metric for £35,000 – is more exciting than talking about free tea and coffee and a company newsletter.

People who talk about receiving a 'package', however, tend to mean the money. They are implying that they are not mere wage slaves, but fat cat types laden down with share-options, pension plans, golden hellos, golden handcuffs, golden parachutes and luncheon vouchers.

In the twelfth century, our forebears went to the Low Countries to sell them wool. They brought back *pac*, a Middle Flemish word for a loose assembly of goods wrapped in a covering. The verb 'to pack' followed.

Originally 'package' meant the act of packing, or the right to pack and transport certain items. Later it became a physical object, somewhere between a packet and a parcel.

The figurative use is American. From the 1840s, the railroads sold 'package tickets', valuable for a number of journeys rather than a period of time. Thomas Cook invented the 'package tour' in the same decade: but he didn't call it that. That happened in the 1950s, by which time 'packages' of intangible goods, ideas, policies and benefits were commonplace.

The unadorned 'package', meaning 'dosh', is a product of Britain's short-lived *Serious Money* era. But anyone still in the habit of boasting about the magnificence of his 'package' should beware. The word has recently acquired a new use, in the smutty magazines aimed at young men and women. It means the male genitalia, especially when gift-wrapped.

Pan out

Traditionally the British buttoned their raincoats against the rain and waited for 'something to turn up'. Recently, though, we have started 'looking at the upside', 'taking a punt' and waiting to see how things 'pan out'.

'To pan out' is a metaphor that came into prominence just as the nation discovered money, first in the 1980s boom and then through the National Lottery. It was highly appropriate, because what actually 'pans out' is gold dust. And all you have to do to get it is spend years knee-deep in a creek, swirling dirty water around in a metal dish.

You will recall from *My Darling Clementine* the 'forty-niners', who led the California Gold Rush. By 1852, things had quietened down sufficiently for one of them to write home, describing for the first time the technique of 'panning out a few basinfuls of the soil'.

By the late 1860s, though, the expression was being used figuratively, and it was immediately spotted by collectors of interesting new expressions. In 1875, *Scribner's* magazine observed that 'A good business is said to "pan out well".'

As the California goldfields dried up, the prospectors moved on to Australia, South Africa and Canada, taking with them their pans (4″ deep and 18″ wide, should you feel like making one) and their vocabulary. In 1892, the *Pall Mall Gazette* in London gave it a try: 'Unfortunately this business did not "pan out", to use the American phrase.'

Since then the phrase has been fully naturalized. What has happened recently, according to some authorities, is that it has changed from slang to colloquialism. Slang is language used by people of whom we disapprove. And until quite recently that tended to include gold-diggers.

Pants

A conversation in a staff canteen: 'What is it today?' asks one young man, near the end of the queue. His friend has been to the front. 'It's pants,' he says, with a grimace.

Health watchdogs can relax. 'Fricassee of Y-front' was off. So was 'roast leg of boxer with all the trimmings'. The young man was providing an opinion, not a description. 'Pants' means 'rubbish'.

But was this some in-joke, or a piece of genuine slang? It seems it's the latter, duly recorded by lexicographers from the mid-1990s. It started in the 'rude' playground humour of children before being popularized by disc jockeys and others who do that kind of thing professionally.

The 'pants' in question are underpants. The same piece of slang could never have arisen in the United States, where 'pants' are trousers and hence not rude at all. This difference can cause confusion, even embarrassment ('Come in just a tee-shirt and pants . . .'). But it is of our own making.

'Pants' is an American diminutive of 'pantaloons', first used in the 1840s. These long, tight breeches, fastening at the ankle or tied under the foot, were common male dress in America in the nineteenth century. Their name came from the French *pantalon*.

That, in turn, is said to come from Pantaloon, a famously trousered Commedia dell'Arte character named after San Pantaleone, a saint beloved in Venice. What more could anyone want to know?

But when pantaloons began to hang loose, turning into modern trousers, the Americans stuck to the old term and its diminutive.

Our 'trousers', on the other hand, were originally a loose overgarment that people wore on horseback, with a name derived from the medieval Irish 'trews'. When 'pants' came along, we used it for masculine versions of what were previously known as 'drawers'. 'Pants' may be funny now, but 'drawers' are in a class of their own.

Paradigm

Here are a few 'paradigms', confidently identified in the newspapers: Daddies' brown sauce; Jarvis Cocker; the fall of Troy; and a man coming home from work, finding someone in bed with his wife, and killing him. What on earth can this word mean?

Literally, a 'paradigm' is an example or pattern: thus Jarvis Cocker is a 'paradigm' of pop stardom. It's effectively a Greek word (giving us that peculiar last syllable, pronounced 'dim' or 'dime') and means all manner of patterns, including architects' models. Plato used it to mean the perfect divine originals upon which all earthly things are modelled.

English adopted it in the fifteenth century for use in philosophical commentary, in rhetoric and in grammar, where it meant a word in all its inflectional forms, for instance, 'eat, eats, ate' and so on.

In our own century, analytical philosophers have used it, in ways that would have made Plato weep. And lawyers use it in defining their terms. For instance, the murder mentioned above is the 'paradigm case', or perfect example, of the defence of provocation.

More influential than these, however, has been the philosopher of science, Thomas Kuhn, whose 1962 *The Structure of Scientific Revolutions* used it to mean a theory or discovery so powerful as to provide the framework for all subsequent work.

This is the source of that expression 'paradigm shift', so beloved of contemporary management. A 'paradigm shift' is the moment when your whole frame of reference changes, for instance when the Cold War ends, when Labour wins a landslide victory, or when your firm decides to get a new letterhead.

The word is not exactly part of the language of the street, nor likely to be. But its ubiquity in academia has made it popular with commentators and journalists, especially those who like to remind their readers that they went to university.

Partner

There's something sick-making about the word 'partner', but we're all going to have to get used to it.

It's officialdom's chosen term for anyone with whom you might be having a sexual relationship, replacing husband, wife, boyfriend, girlfriend, lover, paramour, consort and spouse. But then, many of those people are using it themselves. Voluntarily.

The word comes, somehow, from the medieval Latin *partition-arius*, one who shares. Originally 'partners' shared something – a kingdom, a piece of land – but later they shared an activity, usually dubious: hence 'partners in crime'. After that, for some reason, it came to mean people who went into business together. The King James Bible, for instance, describes James, John and Simon Peter, the disciples, as 'partners' in a thriving Galilee-based fishing enterprise.

Bureaucrats, particularly in education, health and social security, like to use 'partner' in the domestic sense because it is neither 'judgemental' nor 'sexist'. They can ask someone about his or her 'partner' without needing to know whether that person is male, female, spouse, live-in lover or someone they had sex with but whose name they didn't quite catch. This makes it, in the jargon, 'inclusive'.

That's also why traditionalists loathe it: they don't want all relationships, however unconventional or transitory, to be accorded equal respect. 'I don't have a *partner*,' you sometimes hear people snarl. 'I have a *wife*.' Nonetheless, it serves a purpose, as does 'companion', its up-market equivalent.

Besides, 'partner' has been a word for spouse since the eighteenth century, and rather a loving one. It appears in Smollett's 1749 tragedy, *The Regicide* – 'What means the gentle partner of my heart?' – and in Southey's *Poet's Pilgrimage*: 'So forth I set . . . And took the partner of my life with me.'

Without those extra words of definition, however, 'partner' will always be ambiguous. Cowboy films will never be the same again, that's for sure.

Pear-shaped

'I was doing very well at the start,' said the failed greengrocer, 'but then everything went pear-shaped.' To go 'pear-shaped' is to go wrong, amiss, awry or wonky. But why?

The word 'pear' is recorded first at about the time of the last millennium, as *pere* or *peru*, the name coming originally from the Latin *pirum*. Fruit generally have hundreds of symbolic and figurative meanings – consider lemon, plum, peach, cherry – but the pear has always missed out.

It was, however, used in the later Middle Ages in various derogatory sayings. At various times people and things could 'avail not a pear', be 'not worth a pear' or 'as rotten as a pear'. Then in the seventeenth century came the 'pear of confession', described in dictionaries as a 'pear-shaped instrument of torture': luckily no diagram is provided.

So at that stage to be 'pear-shaped' might indeed have been bad. But since then the pear, and 'pear-shaped' things generally, have had an impeccable reputation. 'Pear-shaped' diamonds, for instance, are very popular.

What's more, if you look at art, the 'pear-shaped' figure has always represented the ideal of feminine beauty, catwalk stick-insects notwithstanding.

But in the case of things 'going pear-shaped', the analogy is obviously with things that should be circular or spherical but become distorted. The obvious example is a punctured football, which is a mundane but plausible source for the expression.

But a more disastrous way for things to go 'pear-shaped' is if they are either revolving on an axis or associated with something revolving. It has been suggested that the expression escaped from the world of aviation. A recent aircraft engine was built with an outer casing that was inclined to go 'pear-shaped' in service, with unfortunate effects on the rotating bits inside. Very plausible – and it wasn't even one of ours.

The People

Has Her Majesty's Government lost interest in 'The People'? When it first took office, it talked about little else but 'The People's Europe', 'The People's Lottery', 'The People's Monarchy' and 'The People's Dome'. Perhaps people got fed up with it.

Some claimed to hear in this rhetoric an echo of earlier, more frightening times. After all, isn't the Labour Party the one that has that song about the blood-drenched state of 'The people's flag'? The same possessive construction was certainly favoured in Soviet Russia, Eastern Europe and China. Anywhere, in fact, where the 'People's Police' could haul their opponents before the 'People's Courts' before pronouncing the 'People's Verdict'.

'The People' is quite new in Britain. In the fourteenth century, when the word started being used, Britons aspired to being 'a people', a coherent nation, rather than 'The People'. Anyway, most accepted that they were really their feudal lord's people, or their king's.

It was possible to speak of 'the people', meaning the masses, but with no great political implications. Those came in the seventeenth century, when the King was estranged from 'his people' on a permanent basis. For the first time, Parliament suggested that 'The People', rather than The Crown, might be the legitimate source of authority.

Subsequent radicals and revolutionaries took their cue from that, including the Jacobins in France and the socialists of the nineteenth century. The same went for the American revolutionaries (rebels, as we know them). But they were canny enough to place 'The People' at the heart of their new nation, rather than leaving them outside to throw stones and trample on the flower beds.

So in America 'people' is a popular, patriotic word. Look at their businesses: People's Pharmacy, People's Auto Repairs, People's Funeral Chapel and so on. There are a hundred and thirty-four like that in the California Yellow Pages alone.

We like 'people' too. It's 'The People' we're not sure about.

Petrolhead

Channel Four, which likes to cater for minorities, once announced an evening for 'petrolheads'. Viewers racked their brains. Who are these unfortunates? Why do they need their own programmes? Is there anything on BBC2?

Firstly, a 'petrolhead' is not a 'propeller-head', another phenomenon of our day. The 'propeller-head' is so called because he (and he's always a he) behaves as if he had a propeller on his head. He's a technology fanatic, lifting off the ground with excitement and buzzing around to each new enthusiasm. Think Sir Clive Sinclair.

The 'petrolhead', on the other hand, is more like a 'pothead' or an 'acidhead'. A 'petrolhead' is someone who likes petrol, and the machines that run on it, to the extent of being addicted. Think Jeremy Clarkson.

You've been able to add 'head' to a word to indicate an addiction for most of this century. Here's a book called *White Slavery*, from 1911: 'Opium smokers, "hop fiends" or "hop heads", as they are called, are the fiercest of all the White Slavers,' it states, neatly combining two moral panics in the same sentence, a feat worthy of the *Daily Mail*.

'Pot heads', 'acid heads' and others followed, culminating in the all-purpose, free-standing 'head', used in the mid-1960s to mean a user of drugs and participant in the hippie scene. After that came various '-heads' who were addicted to things other than drugs: 'breadheads', who liked money; 'Deadheads', who liked the Grateful Dead. And now 'petrolheads'.

The Clarksonian 'petrolhead' must not, however, be confused with 'blockhead', 'meathead', 'dickhead' and others less printable. That genre of abuse, first used in the sixteenth century, works by making a simple comparison between someone's head and something unpleasant. They're a way of saying someone is stupid. Whereas 'petrolhead' is saying something more subtle, but perhaps no less damning.

Now
more
Barry
White

Plateau

To plateau

Someone commented a while ago that the listenership of Radio One had 'plateaued'. What an ugly word, and inaccurate too. To 'plateau' must surely mean to reach a high level and stay there, whereas the BBC's pop station has taken quite a different trajectory.

Such a barbarous invention must be new, you might think. Not so: the conversion of 'plateau' from noun to verb is old enough to have become respectable. It is first recorded in 1952 in the *Proceedings of the Society For Experimental Biology & Medicine*. By 1967 it had been accepted by *The Economist*, which talked of a pipeline 'plateauing out'. Now it's commonplace, although familiarity has not made it any more attractive.

The noun 'plateau' (from the Old French *platel*, meaning a flat piece of wood or metal) was an eighteenth-century import, first used in the obvious geographical sense. It owes its present fame, however, to medicine. At the end of the nineteenth century, doctors first began to plot changes in blood pressure as a rising and falling line on paper. To describe what they saw, they spoke of 'peaks', 'troughs' and 'plateaux'.

Things which reach a 'plateau' have tended to be those which can be expressed as a simple line graph: prices, expenditure, the birth rate, the listenership of radio stations. But it has been used entirely figuratively. People are sometimes said to have reached an 'emotional plateau', which doesn't mean they've gone to a bit of high ground populated by people who keep bursting into tears.

For a while in the 1960s, the word enjoyed great notoriety when it was picked up by Masters and Johnson, pioneers of scientific sexology, to describe one of the four phases of the human female's sexual response cycle. The 'plateau' phase is the bit between excitement and orgasm. If it made them feel like that, Radio One would never be short of listeners.

Player

It is perfectly possible to be a 'player' without ever strapping on your boots, dealing a hand of cards or even picking up a musical instrument. And it may well be more lucrative.

A 'player' is a person – or an organization – capable of taking an active part in any situation even loosely analogous to a game. A company can be a 'player' in its market. An Oscar-winning actor may become a 'player' in the game of Hollywood stardom. Britain even likes to be a 'player' in the world of international affairs, although it has to ask the big boys' permission.

This is a new twist for an ancient word, which has a delightful source in the Old Dutch verb *pleyen*, meaning to dance, or leap for joy. The literal meanings of 'player' were established here by the fifteenth century: one who takes part in a game; one who gambles; one who performs on a musical instrument; and one who acts.

According to Shakespeare, ahead of the game as usual, 'All the world's a stage, and all the men and women, merely Players'. This is increasingly true.

Our new all-purpose 'player' goes back to the idea of 'playing' the market as one plays the casino. In the 1980s, it seems to have migrated from Wall Street into the City, business and the media. Inside the financial world, however, it may be older, appearing in a 1934 book on speculation.

Robert Altman's 1992 film, *The Player*, concerning the doomed efforts of a screenwriter to attain power in Hollywood, merely made the word a fashionable synonym for 'operator' or 'major figure'.

It has had other meanings, however. To British soldiers in Northern Ireland during the 1970s, 'players' were terrorists. To male New Zealanders in the 1950s, a 'player' was an available woman. Elsewhere, it seems to have meant a male prostitute and a pimp. They don't tell you that in the *Financial Times*.

Proactive

It's no longer enough to be 'well-motivated', 'bright' or a 'self-starter'. If you want to get on, the thing to be is 'proactive'.

In job advertisements and brochures, 'proactive' seems to mean no more than 'lively' or 'busy'. But it also features in the pronouncements of those running the world, usually from a desk in Whitehall. So it must mean something, mustn't it?

'Proactive' was coined in the 1930s in educational psychology, to describe events that happened in a person's past but continue to have an effect. Our 'proactive' seems to have been borrowed from that, but has a rather different meaning. It appeared in the early 1970s, in a book about policing, and was intended to represent the opposite pole to 'reactive'.

A 'reactive' person or institution is content to 'react to' things – crimes, for instance – after they have happened. The 'proactive' police force, or 'police service', as it likes to be known, doesn't wait for crimes to take place. Instead it acts first, by infiltrating criminal gangs, putting up television cameras and placing cardboard police cars on motorway bridges to discourage speeding.

This ideal of 'proactivity' has since spread to all areas of life, especially commerce, which explains why you currently receive so many unsolicited calls to ask whether you want double glazing, life assurance, children's books or even a will.

Interestingly, 'proactive' couples the Greek prefix *pro-*, meaning before, with a Latin word. 'Active' comes from *agere*, the Latin verb 'to do'. Originally it referred to things 'done before': now it means things you 'do before'. Before your boss finds out you haven't done them, in most cases.

Classically-minded readers may be reminded of what C. P. Scott, legendary editor of the *Manchester Guardian*, said about television: 'No good will come of this device: the word is half Greek and half Latin.' He may have been on to something.

Punter

The secret of success is well known: you give 'the punters' what they want. But who exactly are 'the punters'?

We know 'punter' best as a gambling term. But since the 1980s, when getting rich quick was a popular obsession, it has become an all-purpose synonym for 'customer' or 'member of the public'.

Originally, in the eighteenth century, a 'punter' was someone who 'punted', which was to 'bet against the bank' in various card games. The verb was an Anglicization of the French *ponter*. In Victorian times, 'punter' was applied to gamblers generally, and then to those playing the Stock Exchange.

In late nineteenth-century criminal slang, it was someone who conspired in an auction ring; and in New Zealand it is a pickpocket's assistant. But these are aberrations. Normally, a 'punter' has been a *victim*. It is used of people who buy things off used car dealers and street traders, and is synonymous with 'mug'. It is also used, for some reason, of people who buy lottery tickets.

But perhaps its most consistent use outside gambling has been in the context of street trading of a rather specialized sort. It means someone who uses the services of a prostitute.

In the late 1970s, however, this unpleasant word began to be used more widely, for customers of all sorts. In 1984, for instance, it was recorded as the standard term used by chalet girls to describe the skiers in their charge. The BBC even briefly legitimized 'punters' by making it the title of a dull radio programme, in which Mr and Mrs Average asked boring questions of the authorities and were boringly fobbed off.

Ubiquitous though it is, 'punters' retains a strong undertone of contempt. Perhaps that is what makes it so popular in what are sometimes called the service industries.

Quality

'Quality' is booming in Britain. Every last whelk stall seems to be applying for a 'Quality Mark' or practising 'Total Quality Management'. But does this make the whelks better?

For all the time spent talking about it, 'quality' remains elusive, possibly because the word itself is so slippery. Fundamentally, the 'quality' of something is its 'nature'. The word comes from the Latin *qualis*, meaning 'what kind of?'. In other words, the 'quality' of something is its 'whatness', or, as one dictionary puts it: 'that which makes a thing what it is'.

But a thing's 'quality' is also its degree of excellence, and here ambiguity arises. It is both a relative term ('the quality of your work varies between poor and abysmal') and an absolute one ('this is work of quality').

The vogue for 'quality' reflects British management's recent enthusiasm for things Japanese, with the possible exception of jobs for life and raw fish. Our factories have 'quality control', where a man with a clipboard groans and sends things back. Theirs have 'quality circles', where smiling workers endlessly discuss ways to make things better. Spot the difference.

But 'quality' is also an adjective. From the eighteenth century, the upper classes were called 'people of quality', 'quality people' or simply 'the Quality'. They enjoyed 'quality living', possibly in 'Quality Street' (you can still see them on the tin), and perused 'quality newspapers'. But the word has slipped down the social scale. Today, every High Street butcher offers 'quality meat', and he doesn't mean the stuff they eat at Balmoral.

'Quality' is often contrasted with 'quantity'. Modern parents can't afford to give their children the 'quantity' of time they'd like, because they're always in the office. So they give them 'quality time'. There's not much of it, but it really is excellent.

The same is said of Japanese food. And not everyone believes that, either.

Rage

A 'rage' is an outburst of violent anger. If someone says it's not, kick his head in.

In French, where 'rage' began, *la rage* means rabies. That's how violent it is. It derives from the Latin word *rabies*, which means both extreme fury and the madness of a mad dog.

'Rage' arrived here at the end of the thirteenth century, still carrying those associations. So when Shakespeare said King Lear was in a 'great rage', he didn't mean he was a bit miffed. But English lost the connection with madness, and adopted the Latin word for rabies. But 'rage' kept the fury.

We like to play such things down. So a rage came to mean a strong enthusiasm and even, by the beginning of the nineteenth century, a passing fashion. When 'all the rage' appeared in about 1870, it was used about a parlour game involving hardly any violence.

The mouth-frothing 'rage' has, however, made a comeback. There is 'road rage', in which frustrated motorists attack one another with tyre jacks, axes and screwdrivers. One unfortunate woman even had a live rat thrown through her car window.

And there is 'roids rage', in which bodybuilders full of illegal anabolic steroids started giving impromptu demonstrations of their strength and aggression, sometimes bringing in women and children as their involuntary sparring partners.

In America, a defence of diminished responsibility through 'Black rage', a sudden awakening to oppression, was used by a man charged with shooting twenty-five White commuters. But 'Black rage' is also used of the smouldering career anger cultivated by rappers, some of whom live in Beverley Hills and enjoy a game of golf.

But 'rage' has happier associations. For Australians, and now some British students, a 'rage' is a wild party, and to 'rage' is to go on a spree. 'We were raging last night,' they say, meaning they enjoyed a glass of milk and a game of dominoes before turning in.

Regular

A tourist wanders into an American drugstore and asks for a packet of indigestion tablets. 'Regular?' asks the assistant. 'There's no need to be personal,' blushes the Englishman, mortified.

The American treats 'regular' as a size. The tourist thinks it refers to his digestive tract. It's a good old joke, but young Britons are now as fluent in American as Ronald McDonald.

'Regular' appeared in the fourteenth century, from *regula*, the Latin for 'rule'. At first it was used solely of those bound by the 'rule' of a monastic order. By the seventeenth century, however, it meant things that were symmetrical or ordered: a face, for instance, or a way of life.

The first use of 'regular' to mean 'recurring at fixed intervals' was actually in the *News-Letter* of Boston, New England. In 1756 it promised 'A regular monthly correspondence between Great Britain and His Majesty's several colonies.' The War of Independence broke out almost immediately.

But what about those bodily functions? As long ago as 1807, a report in the *Medical Journal* declared of a patient that 'her bowels were regular'. We are more squeamish now: people are regular, not body parts.

'Regular fellow', meaning 'ordinary, decent chap', is first recorded in America in 1920. Unfortunately, nobody explained it to a visiting G. K. Chesterton, who was mortally offended when a reporter told him he was 'a regular guy'.

'Regular' may also mean 'thorough' or 'absolute'. Your grandmother, for instance, might pat your head and say, 'You're a regular little comedian, aren't you?', apparently not noticing that you are thirty-nine years old and big in derivatives.

In 1942 the American Dialect Society recorded the appearance of 'regular' as a measure of size, noting that it was a euphemism for small.

This was prescient. In today's hamburger restaurants, everything is large, medium or 'regular'. The small 'cola' and the small portion of 'fries' enjoy the same popularity as the small condom.

Relationship

Have you noticed how everyone wants to have a 'relationship' with you these days? If it isn't your bank manager, it's your independent financial adviser or your local supermarket. To say nothing of the milkman and window-cleaner.

In the spiralling sycophancy of contemporary business, forming a 'relationship' with your customers is even more important than telling them to have a nice day. A 'relationship' is so much more intimate than simply providing a service and taking their money.

A 'relationship' is really a matter of kinship or, most commonly, of sexual connection. Not that it is a well-defined term. A 'relationship' implies sex, but not vice versa, as you can discover in any bus queue. 'We sleep together and all that,' you hear young women wail, 'but I'd rather have a relationship.'

A 'relation' is a person to whom you are connected by marriage or birth. Early on, it also meant the connection or kinship itself. Then, in the eighteenth century, the word 'relationship' was created to take on that role. It soon moved beyond the narrow familial and marital field, so that by the nineteenth century it was possible to talk of the 'relationship' between things.

Only in our own time has 'relationship' come to mean primarily a sexual connection. Like 'partner', it is 'inclusive' and 'non-judgemental', because it does not provide those wishing to judge with the necessary detail.

Rolling Stone noted in 1977 that 'people don't fall in love any more, they have relationships'. Since then, affairs, romances, flings, and even marriage have gone the same way.

The commercial use of 'relationship' is a sneaky attempt to introduce some of the warmth and intimacy of romance into the business of selling things. You don't actually have a 'relationship' with any of these people. If you were, you would take their telephone calls.

Result

In a busy office, young men in sharp suits are talking animatedly into telephones. Suddenly one puts down the receiver. 'Result!' he roars, and his colleagues rush to congratulate him.

A lucrative sale has been made, or perhaps a triumph achieved on some more intimate level. The single word 'result!' is enough to indicate success. In contemporary usage, all results are favourable: a 'good result' has become a tautology.

How has this come about? 'Result' is a seventeenth-century noun, adapted from a fifteenth-century verb taken from the Latin *resultare* ('to spring back'). It has always meant 'a consequence or outcome', whether of a scientific experiment, a legal process or a sporting contest. But until now a 'result' could be either good or bad.

Its new meaning, 'a favourable outcome', comes from the occupational dialects of two different worlds. The first is football. As early as 1973, the player Eamonn Dunphy recorded in his diary of a season at Millwall (published as *Only A Game*) that he expected to 'get a result at Blackpool'. Typically, the club lost 1–0, but the expression, at least, was a winner. 'Getting a result' remains an essential of post-match analysis, along with the claim that 'the lads done well' and the admission that it is 'too early to talk about the title'.

The second world is law and order. Prisoners are said to use 'result' to mean a favourable outcome to a request for parole. The police, in contrast, use it to mean 'an arrest' or 'a conviction'. This rich heritage made it a natural for television's *Minder*, that treasure trove of linguistic variety, and from there it spread rapidly to the general population.

Today it is frequently employed by sharp-suited young men, not only for work but in nudging inquiries about romantic matters: 'Well,' they will ask one another, 'did you get a result?'

Retro

Retro

In the 1960s, 'retro' was a noun, meaning a rocket motor used to slow down a spacecraft. Today it's an adjective, meaning something fashionably old-fashioned. This is a measure of the distance we have travelled – and in which direction.

'Retro' comes from the Latin adverb *retro*, meaning 'backwards'. In English it is commonly used as a prefix, appearing first in 'retrograde', coined by Chaucer in his *Treatise on the Astrolabe*, written in the last years of the fourteenth century. He used it to describe planets which appear to move 'backwards' across the skies.

Many more 'retro-' compounds arrived subsequently, including 'retrospect' (first recorded in 1602), 'retroactive' and 'retrocoient', helpfully defined in the *OED* as 'an animal that copulates backwards'. Again, no diagram is supplied.

New compounds are still being added: 'retrofit', to modify something, arrived in 1956. 'Retrovirus' came along two decades later, just in time for AIDS.

The current 'retro', however, should really be *rétro*. It is French, an abbreviation of *rétrograde*. It turned up in the world of fashion in 1973, describing collections that took inspiration from the past. And in 1973, who could blame them?

The 1979 opening of a London shop called American Retro, originally selling second-hand clothes from the US, somehow fostered the impression that the word was American. In 1987, the *Daily Telegraph* confidently reported that the fourteen-year-old French expression was 'the latest word in California's ever-surprising lexicon'.

'Retro' has now gone beyond fashion. It can be applied to anything in a self-consciously old-fashioned style, including food, decor, product design, music and comedy.

There is even something called 'retro-gaming', in which computer enthusiasts use up-to-the-minute computers to play jerky simulations of the very first Space Invader games. The oldest of these – the games, not the enthusiasts – are only about twenty years old. Like nostalgia, 'retro' is not what it used to be.

Rolling

The word 'rolling' is a favourite of modern management, which is constantly 'getting things rolling' and launching 'rolling programmes' when it's not closing things down.

As an adjective, 'rolling' is optimistic and heroic, redolent of wagon-trains and the open road ahead. Expressions such as 'rolling campaign' and 'rolling programme' bring welcome dynamism to the act of letting things carry on under their own momentum. Before the vogue for 'rolling', the same kind of people would have used the word 'ongoing', and everyone else would have sniggered.

'Rolling' has a long history as an adjective, recorded first in relation to dice, in a song of *c*.1500, then to wagons, eyes, seas, thunder, landscape, boiling liquids and just about everything else.

Turning to business, a 'rolling increase' appeared in a 1719 account of international trade. 'Rolling annuities' appeared at the end of the nineteenth century. In the late 1950s came that glorious American euphemism, the 'rolling adjustment', a recession that kills off industries one at a time rather than all at once. Today we also have 'rolling format' radio, which has a similar effect on listeners.

This is all just a tributary of the mighty rolling river that constitutes the verb 'to roll'. French in origin, it is found in the British isles from the end of the fourteenth century: the noun 'roll', meaning a length of parchment in the shape of a scroll, had appeared more than a century before that.

It was the shape of the 'roll' and its practical uses, rather than its possibilities as stationery, which were to dominate. The first record of the verb is in a Scottish epic, *The Legends of the Saints*. There the object being 'rolled' was Saint Agatha, naked on a bed of burning coal.

This puts the torture involved in enduring a 'rolling rationalization programme', for instance, into some kind of perspective.

Rubbernecking

The car radio brings bad news. There's been an outbreak of 'rubber-necking' on the M1 and traffic has come to a halt.

'Rubbernecking' is the common practice of slowing down and craning your neck to see an accident on the opposite carriageway of the motorway. The upshot, usually, is another accident. On your side.

This is fairly new, but the word has been around longer than you might think. In 1896, in his column in the Chicago *Morning News*, the humorist George Ade wrote: 'I stood around there on one foot, kind o' rubber-neckin' to find an opening.'

Ade was one of those peddlers of hot slang who ensure they never run out of new words by making a good proportion of them up: it happens. Whether he heard 'rubbernecking' or invented it, it was a simple and vivid description of a physical action.

Soon, though, it came to imply a type of attitude: nosiness, or idle sightseeing. It arrived in Britain in the 1920s, even making it into the pages of Dorothy L. Sayers, who introduces a character who 'could not waste time rubber-necking round Wilvercombe with Lord Peter'.

So far, so harmless. But by the 1930s, less appealing forms of 'rubber-necking' had been described. Said the *Daily Herald*, of a 1937 marital law reform, 'One of its valuable features will be to deprive the rubber-necks, who gloat over the domestic troubles of their neighbours in the local police court, of their entertainment.'

That wasn't close enough for some. In *Call For Simon Shard*, a 1974 crime novel, one policeman asks another to clear a gruesome crime scene: 'Move the rubber-necks on, back to bed.' This is an accurate reflection of the jargon of the constabulary.

This is probably the source of 'rubbernecking', or at least, of the word. The activity would seem to be as old as humanity itself.

Sexy

Sexy

Everything is 'sexy' these days: issues, ideas, projects, business propositions. Everything, in fact, except sex. Why should this be?

'Sex', in our modern sense, is quite new. Not the act, you understand, but the word. It was a Latin word, one of many borrowed by John Wycliffe for his pioneering English Bible of 1384. He used it in the context of Noah's Ark, referring only to what some people would now call the 'gender' of the animals.

It didn't mean sexual intercourse until well into our own century. 'To have sex' is first recorded in a D. H. Lawrence poem of 1929. 'Sexy', meaning both 'concerned with sex' and 'sexually attractive', had turned up in 1925 but in an odd context. The *Nouvelle Revue Française*, writing about James Joyce, was forced to use the new English word, it said, because there was no French equivalent.

But what of the new, sex-free 'sexy'? In our times it is often heard from City 'suits', but previously it was associated with journalists and those who work with them: politicians, PR execs and advertising people. The best explanation comes from Jonathon Green's *Dictionary of Jargon*, which insists that it was coined by the *Sunday Times* Insight team during the 1960s.

These pioneering investigative journalists used it to describe something that was newsworthy, says Green, 'especially if it involved war, disaster, death or anything suitably violent and/or shocking'.

Can we really pin it on them? Apparently so. In 1950s Australia, 'sexy' was a common slang term of approbation, for instance when talking about cars, motorbikes, engines and so on.

Look at the Insight team in the 1960s, and what do you find? Lots of Australians, notably Bruce Page and Philip Knightley. All in all, this would seem to be one investigation that has reached a definite conclusion.

Shrink

If there's one thing more fashionable than seeing a 'shrink', it's boasting about it.

Once a frightening and hostile term, to be used in horrified whispers, the word 'shrink' has become positively affectionate. Some of today's 'media shrinks' even use the term about themselves, though others use a variety of different expressions.

A 'shrink' can be anything from a psychiatrist or clinical psychologist to a psychoanalyst or psychotherapist: the whole range, in fact, from someone who wants to fill you full of drugs to someone who just wants to fill you full of nonsense. A vague term, then, and hence very useful to the incurious and the confused.

'Shrink' is an abbreviated version of 'head-shrinker'. The verb 'to shrink' is Old English, at least one thousand years old, and originally meant to shrivel, like soft fruit. This is not unlike what happens to a human head in the hands of the ingenious Jivaro tribesmen of Ecuador. They remove the skin, then boil it in a herbal mixture (an opening here for Anita Roddick, perhaps?) until it shrinks to the size of the fist.

Those 'head-shrinkers' were first described in 1926. By the 1950s, the anthropological label had been applied to dedicated workers in the field of mental health, a joke that betrayed considerable unconscious hostility, if not terror. Or so you might think, if you were being analytical about it.

'Shrink' arrived in the 1960s and early 1970s. It is now widespread, especially among those engaging in recreational psychotherapy, and seems largely to have shed the fear and scepticism that once accompanied it.

Oddly, the one service 'shrinks' rarely offer is the painless reduction of a swollen head, usually caused by excessive appearances on daytime television and in the newspapers. There is apparently no connection between 'shrink' and 'shrinking violet'.

Shuttle

It's hard to imagine a word that could describe everything from a desperate diplomatic mission to the Manchester–Bradford coach service, but 'shuttle' will do it.

Once it was just part of a loom. Now, by analogy, it describes anything that travels to and fro without really getting anywhere, from the airport bus to the secretary general of the United Nations.

'Shuttle' is found in Old English texts from around AD 1000, as *sciutil* or *scytel*, meaning dart, missile or arrow. Later it was applied to the tool used in weaving, the crafty Anglo-Saxons having noticed the point on the end.

The transport connection began as a literary conceit by the New England sage Ralph Waldo Emerson, who wrote in 1844 that 'the locomotive and the steamboat, like enormous shuttles, shoot every day across the thousand various threads of national descent'.

Railwaymen everywhere, not renowned for their literary interests, rather liked the idea. In Britain, for instance, an article of 1893 referred to 'a "shuttle service" between Charing Cross and Cannon Street'. Apparently it is expected to arrive very shortly.

World War II gave us 'shuttle bombing' and 'shuttle flights', later adapted for civilian use, sometimes using the same planes. And in the 1973 Arab–Israeli war, Henry Kissinger introduced 'shuttle diplomacy'. Diplomacy has been on the run ever since.

In the 1960s, BOAC compiled a waiting list of three thousand people who wanted to travel on its forthcoming 'lunar shuttle'. The Americans went on to build their 'Space Shuttle'. We lost the list.

The 'shuttle' concept retains a certain glamour, or so the promoters of the Channel Tunnel must have thought as they conjured up the defiant Franglais of 'Le Shuttle'. How many real French words begin with 'Sh'?

That piece of branding has since gone the way of the 'shuttle service' proposed by a hotel in Cyprus, which had to be cancelled due to problems with the donkeys.

Skills

As a nation we have probably never had more 'skills'. Unfortunately, 'skills' are not what they used to be.

For example, there was an item on the radio news about a woman who had never had a job and needed to learn a lot of new 'skills' in order to get one. Chief among these, it emerged, was getting out of bed.

In fact, that's fairly advanced. Increasingly, 'skills' are not technical expertise that we have had to learn and practise. They are abilities we have already acquired, usually without noticing.

In the increasingly pervasive language of self-help, training and management, these are called 'life skills', 'emotional skills', 'core skills' and 'social skills'. They include such things as 'listening', 'flexibility', 'problem solving' and 'working with others'. French polishing, arc welding and needlepoint rarely get a look in.

Is there anything in the word 'skill' to justify this? Indeed there is. 'Skill' is a descendant of the Old Norse *skil*, meaning 'difference', or 'distinction'. In Middle English, from about 1200, it seems to have meant 'reason' or 'intelligence', which is not far from some current uses. But the dominant modern sense, 'expertise', only became established in the sixteenth century.

In our own time, 'skills' is more commonly heard than 'skill', especially in official use. For this we can thank the world of education, which started speaking about 'skills' as early as the 1930s. For some reason 'skills' have always been considered less controversial than 'knowledge' or 'learning'.

Anyone who doubts this need only visit a nursery school, where little children no longer chat, play with Lego and look at picture books. Instead they practise their 'communication skills', their 'motor skills' and their 'pre-reading skills'. Then, at playtime, they practise their 'recreational skills'. It makes you glad to be grown up.

Slap

All across advertisements on the London underground a rash of stickers appears, placed by some ultra-Left sect. 'Slap racists and fascists!' it urges.

'Slap'? It's hardly the language of Leon Trotsky, nor, for that matter, a verb anti-fascists would have used a few years back. Either street politics has become a lot less violent (unlikely) or the word has been on a course of steroids.

In our childhoods, 'slapping' was something you did in the playground if you didn't really want to hurt someone. Parents still use it in this way: 'We don't actually believe in physical punishment. But if James is *very* naughty we *will* slap his legs.'

'Slap' has always been a physical word, but not a terribly violent one until now. It means a nominal blow, with the flat of the hand rather than a fist or a weapon. It's a seventeenth-century import of the Low German *slapp*, said to be onomatopoeic in origin, which you can believe.

The sound is part of the appeal, to those who like that sort of thing. And the blows can be quite gentle: you 'slap' your own thighs, or 'slap' a friend on the back.

Admirers of Benny Hill will remember the old man whose shining pate was repeatedly walloped for comic effect. He is said, incidentally, to be the innocent source of 'slaphead', bane of those suffering hair-loss. A condition, incidentally, that cannot be relieved by the application of 'slap', a theatrical term for make-up now enjoying wider circulation.

In London, strangely, the way to intimidate has always been to underplay your violent intentions. So giving someone a slap, as the stickers suggest, probably means stopping just short of murder.

It's a relief to turn to 'slap and tickle', a 1920s expression meaning 'amorous play'. Make love, not war: perhaps that's what the sticker people had in mind.

Sleaze

Sleaze

In the Major era, when 'sleaze' was everywhere, Terry Major-Ball, brother of the Prime Minister, announced that actually the word meant a type of cloth.

This was considered a typical eccentricity, but he had a point. 'Sleaze', the noun, seems to be a back-formation from 'sleazy', the adjective. And there was, in the early seventeenth century, a type of linen known as 'sleazy', or 'sleasie', supposedly because it was imported from Silesia.

But is that 'sleazy' really the same as our word for something dishonest or dishonourable? It may just be a happy collision between slimy and greasy.

The early history of the word is confused. The cloth 'Sleasie', or 'Slesey', appears first in a dictionary entry of 1670, tying it to 'Silesia'. But the adjective 'sleasie' had been around for years, especially in a figurative sense.

In 1648, for instance, Puritans complained to Parliament about 'vain and sleazy opinions about Religion'. It seems to have meant thin and flimsy, like cheap cloth. It was used in exactly that sense until the late nineteenth century in both Britain and America.

When the word reappeared, in the US in the 1940s, it had acquired a sexual component. From 1941 onwards, we find 'sleazy hips', 'sleazy joints', 'sleazy night clubs' and, finally, in the mid-1960s, we arrive at 'sleaze'.

Mysteriously, 'sleaze' has changed in recent British usage from 'sexual scandal' to 'financial misdemeanour'. In America, where it started, scandals are mostly sexual: financial jiggery-pokery rarely raises eyebrows.

When the Major Government's problems started, they had a sexual aspect. Gleefully, the newspapers turned to the word 'sleaze'. And then, even after the sex had gone away, they stuck with it.

More recently, we have had both the Nolan committee report on standards and a new government. So the word 'sleaze' can safely return to textile history. It can, can't it?

Smart

An advertisement for electronic keyboards makes an interesting claim: 'More and more education research is proving that music doesn't just make you happy, it makes you smart as well.'

Unfortunately, it also shows a lot of children in baggy dungarees, wearing baseball caps back to front. Not 'smart' at all, in the British sense.

This is the American version, meaning 'clever'. But although we have all had that meaning drummed into us since infancy – who doesn't know that Yogi is 'smarter than the average bear'? – we don't much use it.

But those who come into contact with high technology, which is all of us, are learning to love 'smart' devices, those incorporating computer intelligence. These began in the 1970s with the so-called 'smart' weapons, thoughtfully – though not infallibly – designed to steer around women and children en route to obliterating their husbands and fathers.

Then there's the 'smart' card, intended one day to replace credit cards, money, driving licence, medical records and keys. Let us hope it will still scrape snow off a windscreen.

The original 'smart' is rare these days. 'Does that smart?' the school nurse used to ask, as she applied some lurid astringent to your gravel-scraped knee. Since before the Norman Conquest, to 'smart' has been to hurt, in a sharp, stinging way. A 'smart' wound was one that really hurt, as was, in a different way, a 'smart' remark.

Later the word was used to describe people, firstly those who were vigorous and quick and then those who were clever. At the end of the nineteenth century, the Americans carried on using it like that, but we stopped.

Being clever was not enough in those days. To be 'smart' you had to be well-dressed or make mordantly witty remarks. The two were combined in the Edwardian 'Smart Set' who, like 'smart sets' ever since, were elegant, urbane, and quite remarkably dense.

Sorted

They are reading the last rites for 'sorted out'. These days everyone, from the moaning farmers on *The Archers* to the moaning shoppers on *Watchdog*, can be heard saying they want things 'sorted'.

Which is odd, considering the word's background. Not for nothing did the Government choose 'Sorted' as its slogan when it plastered the country with giant posters of young Ecstasy victims.

Baffling to many, this campaign used savage irony against the irony-resistant habitués of the rave scene. To them, 'sorted' meant 'I'm in good shape – because I have a good supply of Class A drugs.' The people in the posters had a good supply too, and they were dead. Hence the irony.

But drugs are glamorous, especially among those who don't take them. 'Sorted!' was soon widespread as an exclamation, equivalent to 'All right!' or 'Great!'

The verb 'to sort' really means 'to arrange or classify' and has done since the fifteenth century: in French *sorte* means 'type'. To 'sort out' was originally to pull an item or items out from a group. In this century it came to mean 'to put right', but now it is heading for extinction.

Oddly, it also means 'to beat up', something that began in World War II, possibly as an import from Australia. There it meant 'to reprimand', either by pulling someone out of a group for a word, or by something more quintessentially Australian.

These senses have now passed to 'sorted', which is now used by people who would be shocked if you told them about the drug connection. What's more, it was prison and criminal slang before that.

The low-life comedy *Minder* brought it to a wider public. 'I'll go and sort this Daley geezer,' said a character in a 1987 episode. Interestingly, 'to sort' something, in the sense of putting it right, is not London at all, but Scots and north country: it appears in Sir Walter Scott. What would he have made of it all?

Soundbite

The 'soundbite' is the death of democracy. Will that do? I can say it differently, if you'd like. What do you mean, 'Let's get Alan Clark'?

It began as a technical expression in American television news. The 'sound bite' was the space left by the reporter so that the ostensible subject of the report could say something. Something short, usually. In 1983, news stations were following one hundred words from the reporter with fifteen or twenty words from the subject. But that was before people's attention spans started to shrink.

Later the jargon was used for speech material edited into a filmed report rather than occurring in an interview. The 'sound bite' is a product of the culture that gave us 'bite-size' chicken pieces. It could just as easily have been 'sound nugget'.

But these days a 'soundbite', as we now call it, means something more. It's not just any old snippet of audio. It should be something pungent or provocative.

In other words, it is a word with verbal impact: whether it means anything is secondary. Here's the *Independent* on the 1988 US presidential election: 'This has been the election of the "sound-bite" ... Through a crafty choice of venues and irresistible one-liners, George Bush has been relentlessly associated on the television news with simple, feel-good themes.'

And was that an accident? Hardly. The 'soundbite' has moved on from off-the-cuff remark to committee-assembled *bon mot*, designed to be picked up and quoted.

Thus a word sometimes used to criticize the glibness of politicians and pundits has been embraced by them as a tool of the trade. 'I prepared my speech to include a number of sound bites,' said one proud MP in 1989, welcoming the television cameras into the House of Commons. Nowadays, few speeches include anything else.

Spam

'Oh no, my mailbox is full of "Spam"!' This *cri de coeur* will baffle those who know 'Spam' only as a tinned meat with wartime associations. But on the Internet it is a menace.

'Spam' is unwanted advertising sent by e-mail. Mailboxes are increasingly jammed with this rubbish, much of it urging you to 'Make $$$$$$!' by sending 'Spam' to other people.

But what has this to do with the meat product? It's a long story. 'Spam' was launched in 1937 by the Hormel company of the US, as Hormel Spiced Ham. Sales were slow until the company held a competition to find a new name.

The new monicker was invented by Kenneth Daigneau, a New York actor, who is said to have invented 'Spam' first and then found a product to match. He won $100. 'Spam' is not an acronym, despite people's best efforts.

In World War II, Nikita Khrushchev credited 'Spam' with saving the Soviet Army from starvation. Nonetheless, its sheer pink ubiquity soon gave 'Spam' less heroic associations.

A 'Spam medal', starting with the 1939–45 star, was one awarded to everyone in a military force, regardless of their individual efforts. The adjective 'spammy', meaning commonplace, mediocre and unexciting, seems a reflection of that. We also have 'spamhead', an unattractive name for a bald person, probably a reference to damp pinkness.

But the Internet 'Spam' comes from quite a different source: 'There's egg and bacon; egg, sausage and bacon; egg and Spam; egg, bacon and Spam; egg, bacon, sausage and Spam; Spam, bacon, sausage and Spam . . .' You know the rest.

Computer students in the US were *Monty Python* fans when no one else there had heard of it. The 'Spam' flooding your Internet mailbox may well be related to the 'Spam' that took over the menu at that little café run by Terry Jones in drag and patronized by singing Vikings. Now, after me: 'Spam, lovely Spam!'

Spice

A reader of the *Daily Telegraph*'s technology supplement told what happened to his little niece when she trawled the Net for pictures of the Spice Girls.

Typing 'Spice' and 'Girls' into uncle's computer, she stumbled upon numerous underdressed women in disgusting and would-be provocative postures. And not all of them were members of the group.

This unfortunate incident took place, according to a follow-up letter, because ' "Spice" is an American term for erotic material.' But is it?

Things are not really so clear-cut. A repeat of the little girl's search led straight to the worrying 'Lynnford Leather and Spice'. This proved to be a shop selling cowboy clothes and the ingredients for Tex-Mex food. But the mucky stuff was only a mouse's twitch away. Not for nothing is it known as the World Weird Web.

Is it just an American thing? Not really. The word arrived in the thirteenth century, from Old French, in the culinary context. But it has always had its figurative aspects. 'Hope is a swete spice withinne the heorte [heart],' says the 1225 *Ancrene Rule*, although what a handbook for hermits would know about that is unclear.

People have been 'spicing' dull bits of writing, by the inclusion of lively or racy anecdotes, since the seventeenth century. Newspapers and books full of the 'spicy' bits have been known for most of the century as 'the spicies'. And agony aunts are inclined to suggest the 'spicing up' of marriage and love life, although not in the way practised by Barry McKenzie. As he found, 'spice' tends to be 'hot', another all-purpose, sex-related term of approbation.

Which brings us back to the Spice Girls. The correspondent who identified the erotic undertones of 'spice' offered this advice to would-be chart acts looking for a name: 'When planning to become a chart-topping act, think ahead!'

Sadly, that would seem to be exactly what the Spice Girls did.

Spin-doctor

When the newspapers and television were sucked into the wonderful whirling world of 'spin-doctors', 'spin' and 'spinning', they left most of their readers and viewers for dust.

So, for those who still care: a 'spin-doctor' is someone who works behind the scenes to ensure that personalities, policies and events are given the best possible interpretation in the media.

The word 'spin' acquired its journalistic significance in the 1970s when reporters, even here in Britain, often put a bit of 'spin' or 'top-spin' on a report. This could mean anything from 'bring out the inherent drama without distorting' to 'make it up', depending on how long your editor wanted to wait for a knighthood.

The analogy is from ball games. A ball with 'spin' may well be more effective than one which has been delivered in a straightforward fashion. The same is supposed to apply to newspaper articles.

But which ball game? Although we always took it as a cricketing analogy, it seems first to have come from the US, where 'spin' lies close to the heart of the mystic religion of baseball. In what is probably not a compliment, 'spin' is also known as 'English'.

Today, journalists rarely put 'spin' on things. They arrive pre-spun from officials and politicians. 'Spin' in this sense was first used in Jimmy Carter's White House, and is now so well known that it has its own sitcom, *Spin City*, as seen on Channel Four.

Those who practised 'spin' soon acquired laudatory nicknames. In 1984, 'spin doctor' appeared: 'doctor' merely means 'expert'. For a while it had competition from 'spinner' – though not 'spinster' – and the sinister 'spin-meister'.

Surprisingly, 'spin' has only recently started to involve a lot of balls. For the first nine hundred years or so, until the seventeenth century, it referred to the process of creating a strong yarn out of a lot of fluff. Today we call that journalism.

Strand

'We have a highly original early evening strand,' boasts the television executive. 'It's a fly-on-the-wall animal decorating game show, starring Zoe Ball.'

In television a 'strand' is what the rest of us call a 'series'. But it's also the conceptual slot into which a series might go. Thus 'our consumer strand' means *Watchdog*. But 'our forthcoming philately strand' means 'our exciting stamp-collecting series, if we make one'.

But what sort of 'strand' is it? The kind people walk along? Or the sort that people disastrously unravel from a woolly jumper?

The word 'strand' came over with the Vikings and meant first seashore, and then any landing place. A good example is The Strand, in London's West End, once a row of fine houses backing on to the River Thames and now a windswept corridor where people gather to sleep and throw away fast-food packaging.

In the north and Scotland, from the thirteenth century, 'strand' was used as a variant on 'stream'. Could a 'strand' be a flowing stream of broadcast inspiration? Unlikely, although admirers of Channel Four's youth programming will note that in Scotland the word also means gutter.

No, it seems that our 'strand' is a fifteenth-century nautical term meaning the individual lengths of yarn in a cable or rope. Later it also meant the threads in a cloth.

Sir Walter Scott wrote of the 'three strands of a conversation' in 1816, self-consciously remarking that he was using 'the language of rope-work'. The same forgotten metaphor lies behind 'strands of an argument' and 'strands of the plot'.

The television 'strand' is a metaphor too, suggesting a single thread of content forming part of the vibrant, multi-hued fabric of a modern television channel. To mere viewers, however, it may sound more like an admission that money spent on television is money for old rope.

Stress

It is the all-purpose modern ailment. 'He's off work with stress,' you hear people say. Or, among those still at work, 'I'm stressed.'

'Stress' means both 'pressure', and an adverse reaction to that pressure. So if you mention the 'stress' in the office, make it clear that you're talking about the former. That way you'll be taken for a captain of industry rather than a hypochondriac.

The word has always had this ambiguity. 'Stress' began life as a fourteenth-century variant on 'distress'. It meant the experience of physical hardship, starvation, torture and pain. But it also meant causing hardship. 'Another villainy there is, to do a woman sin through stress,' wrote Robert Brunne in 1338, who wasn't talking about making her work late.

From the fifteenth century, the word became almost a synonym for weight: both physical weight and metaphorical weight, meaning the sense of the emphasis in an argument. It was also adopted by grammarians to mean the weight placed on individual syllables.

In the nineteenth century, mechanical engineers redefined the word as a technical term. 'Stress' meant the pressure on an object. This was contrasted with 'strain', the deformation experienced by an object under 'stress'. Borrowing that would have clarified things: 'He's had a lot of stress, so he's off with strain.'

Unfortunately, psychologists and doctors in the 1940s began using 'strain' to mean both circumstances capable of disturbing a person's equilibrium and their reaction to those circumstances. But strictly speaking, 'stress', unlike 'anxiety' or 'worry', had to cause increased secretions of certain hormones, notably adrenaline.

These days, however, the term is bandied around so imprecisely that we are almost back to the medieval definition, in which 'stress' means nothing more precise than 'pressure'. Let us hope that no one suggests any medieval cures for it.

Survivor

Among the declared aims of the Diana, Princess of Wales Memorial Fund was to help 'survivors'. Historically, for there to have been 'survivors', someone has to have died.

But today the word includes those who have survived only in the sense of carrying on after bad experiences. Which is a lot of people.

The reason 'survivors' requires someone else to die is because 'to survive' means 'to outlive'. That's what *survivre* meant in French before arriving here in the fifteenth century.

In law, 'a survivor' is someone who outlives a co-owner or co-tenant. In America, the word is used in pensions and life insurance documents, as an 'inclusive' alternative to 'widow', 'widower' or 'surviving cohabitee'. But it looks awfully stark to us.

The verb 'to survive' has not required anyone to die since the sixteenth century. Shakespeare speaks of people surviving shame or treachery. Later writers speak of surviving a journey – even before the advent of rail privatization.

But the noun 'survivor' has generally applied only to people who had actually been in the presence of death. In the 1960s, psychologists treating those who had suffered in concentration camps began using the term 'survivor syndrome' about the terrible guilt experienced by those who lived on while others perished. 'Survivor' thus entered therapy, where it was soon in less careful hands.

It has since been taken up by those treating people who have experienced child abuse, mental illness, eating disorders and more. It is undoubtedly popular with 'survivors', because, unlike victim or patient, it sounds heroic.

Also, it has a Karaoke-friendly theme tune, made famous by Gloria Gaynor but now shockingly popular with anyone who has ever had a bad time, preferably with a man. To get the benefit, you have to be able to hold a drink and a microphone, but not necessarily a note.

Syndrome

If it sometimes seems as though there's another 'syndrome' invented every minute, that's because there is. A 'syndrome', unlike a disease or a disorder, is something lots of people are qualified to diagnose.

Although it started life as a medical term, meaning a group of symptoms stemming from a single illness, it has long since moved on. The word is Greek, derived from two words meaning 'run' and 'together', and was dragged into English in 1541 by Robert Copland, translator and printer, in a book called *The Questyonary of Cyrurgyens*, which attempted to explain the theories of Galen, the Greek physician.

Four hundred years later, Aldous Huxley, who had some medical background, employed 'syndrome' in a new sense, to mean a characteristic set of opinions or behaviour. In his 1955 novel *The Genius and the Goddess*, he describes a character who takes a professional interest in caterpillars and creepy-crawlies as having 'Gloom-Tomb syndrome'.

Today, 'syndrome' is a word of considerable ambiguity. It describes conditions of impeccable medical pedigree, such as Guillain-Barré syndrome or Acquired Immune Deficiency Syndrome. It can describe a psychiatric condition, such as Munchausen's syndrome by proxy.

Or it can describe some social trauma or set of emotions, such as empty nest syndrome, or famous father syndrome, painstakingly researched by an academic, or dreamt up by a journalist with half a page to fill.

Alternatively, it can just be a joke, like the Pre-Millennium Syndrome currently sweeping the country. Because of this ambiguity, those looking for public sympathy are advised to have their complaint defined as a 'disease' or a 'disorder'.

But calling it a 'syndrome' has its advantages. Because it consists of a lot of different symptoms, a 'syndrome' can be experienced by a lot of different people. So while chronic fatigue syndrome and total allergy syndrome have struggled to enter the medical textbooks, neither ever found it difficult to build a support group.

Synergy

The unfortunate individual sent to explain to the fans why BSkyB wanted to buy Manchester United Football Club was not exactly speaking their language. 'There is a natural synergy,' he insisted. The same synergy, perhaps, as exists between a hungry fox and a plump chicken.

'Synergy' has become part of the euphemistic armoury of the City, where it is used to dress up takeovers as happy marriages between two organizations with everything in common. Previously they might have been called mergers, but people nowadays know that a merger is just a takeover on its best behaviour.

'Synergy' comes originally from two Greek words, *syn*, meaning together, and *ergon*, meaning work. And that is exactly what it means.

But before 'synergy' came a Latin term, *synergia*, much bandied around in the religious controversies of the sixteenth century. Did man and God work together in the act of conversion? Or was it – the orthodox view – all God's doing?

The Latin *synergia* was translated as 'synergie' or 'synergism', a word adopted by medicine in our own century to describe the way certain drugs work together. It can also mean people working together, but 'synergy' won that role, possibly because of its subliminal hint of 'energy'.

'Synergy', too, has a medical history. It means the way in which various bodily organs and mental faculties work together. But from the 1960s, management theorists and the like fell upon it to explain their big ideas. There is, for instance, the '2+2=5 effect', which shows that a) organizations are greater than the sum of their parts, and b) you don't need arithmetic to theorize about management.

Only in the 1980s did 'synergy' find itself part of the verbal toolkit of every City acquisitions expert and PR wizard. With every self-respecting conglomerate, newspaper, sweetshop and rock band now poised to acquire a football club, we can expect to hear more of it.

System

Anything more complicated than a paper clip is now a 'system': from the 'hair care system' that used to be shampoo, to the Post Office 'queueing system' that used to be a disorderly collection of pensioners, and still is.

The word 'system' is intended to imply technological sophistication beyond the reach of ordinary grooming products. Or it is intended to suggest a high degree of organization in something that is self-evidently chaotic. The 'education system', for instance, or the 'self-clear system' in staff canteens.

The commercial use of the word is a hangover from the 1970s and 1980s, when it was applied to complex cameras, hi-fi and video equipment rather than soap. It remains very common in computing, where discussions of 'operating systems' can become quite heated, except when normal people are present.

In origin, 'system' is not a technological word. It derives from the Greek *sustema*, meaning anything from a government or constitution to a musical interval. It arrived in English in the early seventeenth century. Thomas Hobbes used it in *Leviathan*, 1651, of people in business together.

Then in *An Essay Concerning Human Understanding*, of 1690, John Locke mentioned 'this little Canton, I mean this system of our Sun', creating an astronomical term that has lasted to this day. Almost every other science and engineering discipline borrowed it: from primitive medicine to the first 'systems' linking computer programs.

But the word has always had another meaning: an organized scheme of knowledge and belief. We say that Marx built a powerful 'system', but that doesn't mean he spent his weekends fiddling with disco equipment. Actually, he wanted to smash 'The System'. That term, for the oppressive nature of society, appeared in 1806, 12 years before he was born.

When today's young people talk about 'smashing The System', however, they tend to mean that they dropped their shampoo in the shower.

Talent

To most of us, 'talent' is something you *have*: an ability or aptitude. But in show-business, 'talent' is what you *are*: it's your job description.

Television, in particular, is built on the tension between the 'suits', who hold the power, and 'the talent', which tends to mean those who can read an autocue, from Sarah Dunant to Tinky-Winky.

When television people talk about 'talent', they are not making a value judgement. It is perfectly possible to be both 'talent' and extremely 'talentless', as a Saturday evening with BBC1 will quickly demonstrate.

'The talent' have a natural affinity with money. That's because a talent (*talentum* in Latin) was a measure of weight in precious metal. Remember Jesus' 'Parable of the talents'. A man gives five talents to one servant, two to a second, and one to a third. The first two put the money into ISAs, unit trusts and the like and give back the capital plus interest. The third buries it in the ground, and Jesus denounces him.

The meaning of Our Lord's brief spell as an Independent Financial Advisor has never been exactly transparent. Nonetheless, the parable gave us our modern sense of 'talent'. From the sixteenth century, writers in English used the word to mean a gift from God, carrying certain obligations. Later it became simply a term for native ability, with fewer strings attached.

At the start of the nineteenth century, when irony was new, the word was first applied to people. Lord Grenville formed a Government which became known as 'The Administration of All The Talents' because it was so hopeless. You had to be there.

There is also the slang 'talent', used to mean a potential sexual partner. This military expression of the 1930s was first used by men about women. Today it is used by either sex, about either sex.

Does this attitude to 'talent' have anything to do with the way television presenters are chosen? What do you think?

The dog's

A blackboard outside a restaurant ends with the exhortation: 'Come on in – it's the dog's.'

Not very enticing, especially when you know which part of the dog the restaurant is said to resemble. The blackboard is using a politely truncated version of the real expression, 'the dog's ********' or, if you prefer, '********'. Either spelling is acceptable. In other words, the dog's testicles.

And the dog's ******** are suddenly a byword for excellence. This is new, although dogs have enjoyed a rich life in slang for many years. Think of 'a dog's dinner' or 'a dog's breakfast'. Think of a 'dog's body', a nineteenth-century term for an unappetizing ship-board meal, then a low-ranking officer and now someone who does your photocopying.

The versatile animal's private parts have received more than their fair share of attention. Young journalists in the 1970s learned that there were two words for the exclamation mark: 'screamer', by reason of its function, and 'dog's ****', by reason of its appearance. No one ever used it – it was a hot-metal thing – but we were amused that it existed.

But that was only half the story. According to several dictionaries of slang, one dating from 1995, there was a similar expression, used for a slightly less common typographical device: (:–)

Yes, it was the 'dog's ********' again. But that does not explain why that has suddenly become a byword for all that's great, a contemporary version of 'the bee's knees' – and about as meaningful.

There is this clue. In low-life circles in the 1920s, if something was obvious, it was said to 'stick out like the dog's ********'. There is only a short mental leap from something sticking out to its being as 'outstanding' as our restaurant.

Increasingly, though, people say 'the dog's' and omit the rest. It's almost polite enough to use at a dinner party. 'Have you tried the pâté?' you can hear your hostess saying. 'It's the dog's.'

Top

Some young men are in a pub. 'Top man!' they chorus, when one buys a drink. 'Top story!' they chortle, when someone tells a joke. A 'top evening' all round.

'Top' means excellent or eminent, and this is how it is used in the media, which are full of 'top stories' and 'top politicians'. But to anyone young and cynical, the word has an ironical twist.

Its association with the tabloids, and the more witless types of advertising ('Top breeders recommend . . .'), has made it a word that 'media-literate' young people can't take seriously. So they use it to praise something – but in a way that suggests they don't necessarily believe it. This is invaluable at an age when earnest opinions are not required.

Viz magazine's 'Top Tips', for instance, are an absurd parody of the household hints you get in women's magazines. When a writer calls Ronnie Wood 'that top guitarist and bon viveur', he doesn't necessarily mean it as a compliment.

And when laddish magazines drone on about 'top birds', 'top crumpet' and all the rest, they are wallowing in voyeurism while insisting that they don't really *mean* it, just in case anyone should mistake them for the kind of people who have imaginary girlfriends.

The noun 'top' goes back to the Teutonic origins of English, and originally meant the hair on someone's head, or the top of a hill. Only in the seventeenth century did it have anything to do with quality or success.

The adjectival 'top' was late arriving. People tended to use compound nouns – 'top-branch', 'top-people' and so on – even into our own century. Here's Jeremy Collier's *Short View of the Immorality of the English Stage*, a 'top-seller' of 1697: 'These Sparks [fops, or dandies] generally marry the Top-ladies.'

Change the verb and he could have been writing for *Loaded*.

Totty

A roving camera scans the streets of a seaside town. 'Take a look at that totty!' says a lascivious voice. A woman's voice.

What is going on? Women don't talk about 'totty', do they?

They do now, in just the same way they talk about 'talent' or 'a doll', or 'a bit of stuff'. Vulgar male expressions are being turned on those who coined them almost as quickly as they appear.

The thing about 'totty' is that it's only just been given a new lease of life in men's magazines and bars and offices, having spent years on the feminist hit list. Now it's been appropriated, turning the would-be 'totty'-hunter into the hunted, and vice versa. No wonder there's a crisis of masculinity, at least in the *Guardian*.

'Totty' (sometimes 'tottie') seems to have come into use first in Scotland, as a word for a small child: it appears in *Ivanhoe*, for instance. It is a variant on 'tot', which arrived in the eighteenth century, possibly from Iceland (the country, not the freezer centre).

Like 'babe', it soon became a word for woman or girl, and probably one with an approachable nature. Some authorities claim it was a nineteenth-century term for 'high-class whore', but in the twentieth century it has generally been more affectionate than that. In James Joyce's *Dubliners*, for instance, published in 1916, a schoolboy shyly admits that he has 'three totties', and there's no suggestion that he's living off immoral earnings.

After that, the word disappeared, surviving only in forces' slang. From there it seems to have found its way back into the men's magazines, the publishing phenomenon of our age, along with a lot of equally antique social attitudes. Now 'totty' is being deployed by women to objectify, demean and belittle men. No doubt revenge is sweet.

Trademark

'Oh look, here comes Jim in his trademark plastic sandals.' It is hard to imagine anyone saying that, but we *read* it all the time. Here is the *Guardian* on Martin Bell: 'Aged 57, and easily recognisable with his trademark lucky white suit'.

'Trademark', used in this adjectival way, is journalese: language that only appears in the media. The noun 'trade-mark', or 'trade mark', goes back to the sixteenth century, and has been enshrined in the law since 1862.

It is a visual device used by a firm to distinguish its work from anyone else's. Recent 'trade-marks' have included colours and even gestures: two taps on the side of the nose, for instance, now belong to the Derbyshire Building Society. It is welcome to them.

It is possible to use 'trade-mark' in a figurative way to mean the particular distinguishing mark of a person: 'Elaborate practical jokes were Jones's trade-mark.' The adjectival 'trademark' compresses such sentences for reasons of journalistic pseudo-urgency.

It is first recorded in 1977, in the *South China Morning Post*, referring to James Stewart's 'trademark drawl'. In 1983, the *Daily Telegraph*'s fashion pages, a laboratory for linguistic experimentation to this day, remarked that a designer's 'trademark French rayon jersey made up at least half the collection'.

Well, nouns turn into adjectives all the time, and society's foundations have yet to crumble. But if the word is to be used, it ought to be used meaningfully. Martin Bell's white suit is genuinely distinctive, but a lot of journalists seem to think 'trademark' just means 'habitual'.

Here's the *Guardian* again, on Roger Freeman, sometime Chancellor of the Duchy of Lancaster: 'with his trademark double-breasted pin-stripe'. But if it is a 'distinguishing mark' for a Tory minister to wear a double-breasted pin-stripe suit, I am Jean-Paul Gaultier.

Tragic

Anyone who reads the newspapers will have a fair idea of what constitutes a 'tragic mum', or a 'tragic tot'. But what on earth are 'tragic shoes' and a 'tragic hairstyle'?

'Tragic' comes, of course, from 'tragedy', a fourteenth-century English adaptation of the Greek word *tragoidia*. Apparently that word was formed from two nouns, *tragos* meaning 'goat' and *oide* meaning 'song'.

But what made the darkest and most profound of literary forms a '*goat-song*'? Indeed, do goats sing? The Roman poet Horace had an answer. He suggested it was because the poems that became Greek tragedy were written for song contests in which the prize was a goat, rather than a perspex trophy and the chance to host the competition next year.

When 'tragedy' appeared in English, it meant a poem or tale of 'prosperity for a time that endeth in wretchedness', as Chaucer put it. Today we sometimes hear pedants, enraged by a surfeit of 'tragic deaths' and 'tragic journeys' in the newspapers, demanding that the word should only be reserved for discussions of the literary form.

They are, however, four hundred years too late. 'Tragedy' was used of unhappy events in real life as early as the sixteenth century. 'Tragic', the adjective, arrived at about the same time and has never been used solely for fictional matters.

In our own time, 'tragic', like 'sad', is increasingly used to mean 'deplorable' or 'pitiful' – with a touch of contempt. Thus a 'tragic haircut' is not a style that makes the wearer look like Oedipus, but one that makes him look silly.

Partridge's *Dictionary of Slang* pinpoints the arrival of 'tragic' as a term of abuse to *c*.1979, in the Midlands, when a new football chant appeared: 'We all agree, Nottingham Forest are magic.' Which the rival fans, with their usual wit, would modify to: '. . . are tragic'.

This sounds unlikely, but so does the story about the goat.

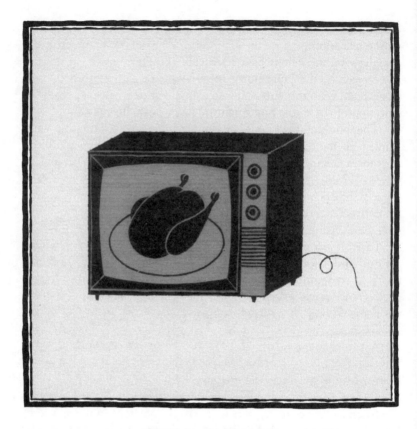

Turkey

Turkey

Do you have 'turkey' at Christmas? Almost certainly, if you switch on the television.

Show-business flops have been called 'turkeys' since the 1920s. More recently, the expression has been extended to worthless things in general. Why this should be so remains a mystery, unless it is a reflection of the edible bird's ugliness and ungainliness.

The 'bootiful' fowl itself has a rather peripheral relationship with Turkey. In the early sixteenth century, the 'turkey-cock' was a bird, African in origin, that was thought to have come via Turkey on its way to Europe. Explorers who arrived in Mexico in 1515 found a vaguely similar bird there, both domesticated and running wild, and for convenience called that 'turkey' as well. It was even given the same Latin name: *meleagris.*

Later it became clear that the two fowls were different. The African bird became known by its alternative name, the 'guinea-fowl', in recognition of a new account of its origins, from Guinea in West Africa via Portugal. The American bird, however, retained the name 'turkey'. It is this impostor that slumps on to our tables at Christmas.

At some point in the early nineteenth century, the expression 'talk turkey' appeared in America, meaning 'to say pleasant things'. More recently, however, the expression has altered to mean 'to talk frankly', or even, 'to say unpleasant things'.

Later in the century, a new 'turkey' appeared in the US and Australia. It was a rough bag carried by tramps, hobos and itinerant workers. Could this unappealing bundle of rags and bones have given its name to unappealing films and plays?

Who knows. 'Turkey' in the modern sense seems to have arrived fully formed in the 1920s. Groucho Marx, in a letter of 1939, complained that 'The boys at the studio have lined up another turkey for us.' He wasn't talking about the catering arrangements.

Tweak

To 'tweak' is to employ the gripping, twisting motion favoured by traditionalist schoolmasters when confronted by children's noses and ears. But these days it has more appealing uses.

Shakespeare used the verb, in exactly this sense, in *Hamlet*. The eternal schoolboy, you will recall, demands, 'Who calls me villain? ... Tweaks me by the nose?' in one of his big soliloquies. It was a dialect word, 'twick', before that, and derived originally from the Old English *twiccian*, to pluck.

Later, Ben Jonson added a noun. In *The Silent Woman* of 1609 he mentioned 'tweakes by the nose, sans numbre'. Charlotte Brontë introduced an innovative 'tweak of the ear' in *Jane Eyre* (1847).

The Jacobeans also used 'tweak' to mean whore. But with the Victorians, the word's innocence returned. In school stories, to 'tweak' was to hit someone with a shot from a catapult, or 'tweaker'.

By the 1930s, 'tweaking' was spin-bowling, something that combined gripping and twisting with arcane skills. Today it means to improve by adjustment or simple modification, which may involve both aspects of the spin bowler's craft.

The modern use is recorded as early as 1966, when *Punch* mentioned someone with a Morris 1100 'tweaked so it'll do nearly 100'. Proof that the magazine did once contain jokes.

Thereafter, 'tweaking' spread to cameras, hi-fi and computers. It has even applied to the workings of the economy, which have been known to need the odd adjustment. In hi-fi magazines the word 'tweak' has become a not altogether kind epithet for those who like to fiddle: a dialect version of 'anorak', if you like.

Meanwhile, in American drug culture, to 'tweak' is to exhibit withdrawal symptoms. The word is said to be a representation of what that feels like. On the whole, you'd do better to stick with the Morris 1100. You might get 105 out of it.

Up to speed

Are you keeping up? Are you on the case? Are you 'up to speed'?

Then perhaps you could explain what 'up to speed' actually means. We know it means 'apprised of the relevant information'. And we know it's a metaphor, but based on what?

It's said to be American, from politics or business. But that's all we know. It is based upon some machine, or process, that must be 'up to speed' to work properly, but that hardly narrows it down.

We might be talking about a lathe, a rotary press, or an electrical generator, which has to be 'up to speed' to produce AC at mains frequency. Or it could be an industrial motor, brought 'up to speed' gradually to overcome inertia. We all know that feeling, and people claim to have heard the metaphorical sense as long ago as 1951.

Then again, users of the expression – politicians, journalists – aren't the heavy industry type. Gramophone turntables, film cameras and sound gear, the hardware of old-fashioned broadcasting, all have to be 'up to speed' before work starts. So that's another plausible source.

Meanwhile, many people have suggested an RAF connection. An aircraft must be 'up to speed' at take-off, and so do the gyroscopes in instruments. Some claim to have spotted the metaphor in this context as long ago as the Great War, although written proof is missing.

A competent secretary or PA undoubtedly needs to be 'up to speed', and not only with shorthand. And one final possibility, which has aesthetic appeal at least, is that 'up to speed' has a musical source. To be 'up to speed' is to be able to play a piece at the indicated tempo. You can imagine the reaction of Beecham or Solti on discovering that some members of their bands were not 'up to speed' at final rehearsal.

In this case, your guess is as good as mine, if not better.

Virtual

The word 'virtual' is now so ambiguous that a 'virtual war' could mean anything from an outbreak of armed conflict to a lot of students playing computer games. Such words need watching.

Until recently, most people used 'virtual' as an adjective meaning 'almost'. But it really means something that exists in all essentials but perhaps not in some technicalities: a 'virtual war', for instance, is really one that hasn't been declared.

Derived from the Latin *virtus*, 'virtual' originally meant powerful or effective. Early Anglicans posited the 'virtual presence' of Christ in the bread and wine of Communion, as opposed to the 'real presence' of Catholicism. The faithful would receive the 'virtue' (or power) of Christ, but not His substance. Thus 'virtual' came to mean 'in essence'.

Confusingly, in eighteenth-century optics a 'virtual image' was something you could see, for instance in a mirror, but which didn't exist. Now, though, physicists speak of 'virtual particles', which you can't see but which *do* exist. This scientific confusion may be connected with Heisenberg's uncertainty principle, but it's difficult to be sure.

In the early 1960s, 'virtual' described computer features that appeared to exist physically but were really only in software, for instance 'virtual memory' and 'virtual disks'. Today it often indicates an electronic version of something mundane. You can go 'virtual shopping', although M&S is still a better bet if you want something that fits. 'Virtual reality', meanwhile, promises one day to immerse us in a simulated world, but concentrates for the time being on helping us blast aliens.

Management theorists, meanwhile, propose the 'virtual company', whose functions (employing people, for instance) are dispersed, but whose 'essence' somehow remains. 'Virtual jobs', it seems, may be the future for all of us. Let's hope our 'virtual wages' are sufficient to pay for our real groceries.

Vision

Vision

Once upon a time someone who admitted to a 'vision' was either an Old Testament prophet, a religious mystic, or mad. Nowadays, he's likely to be your managing director.

Every modern, go-ahead organization now has a 'vision', expressed in something called the 'vision statement'. You may recall the 'mission statement': the 'vision statement' is the same thing, but in drag.

Whereas the 'mission statement' addresses harsh realities, the 'vision statement' is about 'values'. So while your 'vision statement' might declare, 'Our aim is to achieve world peace', your 'mission statement' would be forced to admit, 'We supply heavy artillery to the world's emerging countries.'

In everyday life, 'vision' is an interesting word because it means both something you can see, and something you can't. But this is not a modern confusion: it has been there from the start. The Latin root *visio* means both 'something seen' and 'an idea or notion'.

First recorded in English in 1290, the word was used mainly for the supernatural experiences of saints and prophets. In the fifteenth century, it was first used of the act of seeing, and by the eighteenth century was a preferred term for discussing sight in its scientific aspects. Hence, eventually, television.

The supernatural sense was modified in time to include anything imagined with particular vividness. You might have a 'vision of wealth' or a 'vision of loveliness', a flattering expression now mainly used of the likes of Julian Clary.

In 1926, Fowler's *Modern English Usage* noted that 'vision' was enjoying quite a vogue 'in the sense of statesman-like foresight or political sagacity'. This 'vision thing' was what George Bush famously failed to tackle.

Modern managers will make no such mistake. 'Vision statements' are now ubiquitous, the creation of touchy-feely 'visions' being so much more enjoyable than actually managing anything.

Whatever

At Paddington station, a man asks the price of a ticket. A trick question, of course. But as he starts to explain his itinerary, as you do nowadays, the clerk waves his hand dismissively, punches the button on his machine, and says, 'Whatever.'

What he meant, presumably, was 'On this rare occasion the price of the ticket is not determined by what return train you catch.' But he couldn't be bothered with that rigmarole, so 'whatever' had to do.

This 'whatever' is a recent arrival from the US, where one young enthusiast, writing in the magazine of the University of Arizona, acclaimed it as 'the key phrase of our generation' because it 'implies a disregard that is beyond mere contempt or dismissal'. A natural for railway station staff, then.

In contemporary American usage, the same 'whatever' is the appropriate response to most everyday inquiries, from 'Do you take sugar?' to 'Have I told you about my entire family being abducted by aliens?'

It was popularized in the 1995 film *Clueless*, whose heroine is an object lesson in smug self-obsession. Its note of contempt also made it the ideal title for an early song by Oasis.

'Whatever' has been around for six centuries, but it has not previously constituted a phrase on its own. But in America, 'whatever' has been used since the 1960s as a kind of verbal shorthand. You hear it in their television reporting. 'Whatever, debate is still raging,' they will say, whereas we might say, 'Whatever the merits of this particular case . . .'

The free-standing 'whatever' is more economical still. 'It's like giving someone the bird without even expending the effort to raise a middle finger,' wrote the Arizona student. Do you think he's ever been to Paddington Station?

Wimp

Until recently, English was full of words for challenging someone's manhood. Then 'wimp' arrived and sent most of them packing, a surprisingly thrusting and vigorous performance.

It is recorded in America as long ago as 1966, in the expression 'He's a real wimp on a date.' In the macho 1980s, when lunch was for 'wimps', it became ubiquitous.

Earlier, though, 'wimp' was used by Cambridge undergraduates to denote 'young woman or girl'. There was even a naughty verb, 'to go wimping'. But by 1930, 'wimp' had gone. When it came back it had undergone a sex change and moved to America.

To add to the mystery, there was a 'wimp' in America at the same time as it was in Cambridge. The columnist George Ade used it, of a male, in one of his 'fables in slang', collected in 1920: 'Next day he sought out the dejected Wimp.' But then the 'Wimp' went missing again.

Our modern 'wimp' may just be Wimpy, the ineffectual sidekick of Popeye, whose strip started in 1929. Or it may be some relation of 'whimper'. No one really knows, not even Jean Aitchison, Rupert Murdoch Professor of Language and Communication at Oxford, who is surprisingly knowledgeable about 'wimps'.

Her interest is in how we learnt what the incoming 'wimp' meant, since no one ever explicitly told us. According to *How To Handle Wimps*, her 1995 paper for *Folia Linguistica* (not one of Mr Murdoch's learned journals), it was by observing the context in which this 'new lexical item' was used in newspapers. Knock me down with a feather, to use a 'wimpish' expression.

'Wimp' is also WIMP. That's the 'Window Icon Mouse Pointer' system of working a computer. But it's also the 'Weakly Interacting Massive Particle'. Named by a humorous group of Californian physicists in 1977, these WIMPs are 'the dark matter closing the Universe'. So while God may not actually be a WIMP, He knows where they live.

Wired

Wired

The American magazine *Wired* decided it needed a London edition to galvanize sleepy Britain with hot news from the wild frontier of technology. Instead, it died a lingering death on the shelves of W. H. Smith.

Despite that setback, *Wired* thrives in the US, and the word 'wired' is here to stay. The magazine's readers liked to think of themselves as 'the wired', a tiny technological élite who will soon run everything while the rest of us dish out the fries at McDonald's.

In less all-embracing terms, to be 'wired' is simply to have a connection to the Internet. Hence there are 'wired houses' and 'wired schools', but there are also 'wired women', 'wired lawyers' and 'wired farmers', all connected to the network by a cable – the 'wire' in question.

When the word appeared, a thousand years ago, 'wire' was a valuable commodity, the thread of precious metal used in making jewellery. This explains why medieval and Renaissance poets habitually compared their loved one's golden locks to 'wire'. Do not try this at home.

Only later did 'wire' become mere hardware, suitable for fencing in cattle, conducting electrical experiments or stringing up puppets. From these sprang various figurative expressions: 'to be a live wire', meaning to be full of energy; 'to be on wires', meaning to be jumpy or nervous.

This may be the source of another recent use of 'wired', which provided the title of a 1984 book about the fast life and early death of the comedian John Belushi. To be 'wired' is to be under the influence of drugs, especially cocaine.

Borrowing from that, people sometimes speak of feeling 'wired' when they are simply under stress. The kind of feeling you get, in fact, when you spend hours crouched over a computer, struggling to join the technological élite.

Wonk

When William Hague suddenly emerged as leader of the Conservative Party, he was an unknown quantity. Someone suggested he was a 'wonk' – which only made things worse.

In the parlance of contemporary American politics, and increasingly our own, a 'wonk' is someone who is seriously interested in the detail of political life: a person whose idea of heaven is a nice thick paper about pensions or VAT without so much as a television appearance at the end of it. A 'policy wonk' is the same, only more so.

This 'wonk' was first spotted in 1962, in *Sports Illustrated*, the Bible of American machismo. It was a disparaging term for a swot, a nerd, or what is now sometimes called a wuss, and seems to have been college slang. Erich Segal, a college professor as well as a purveyor of glutinous romance, used it in his *Love Story*.

Where did it come from? Some have observed that it is 'know' backwards. Which is true, but hardly relevant. The brief vogue for backslang ended at least 100 years ago, leaving us with a single useful word: 'yob'.

There are more convincing options. In the slang of Australian Aboriginals, a 'wonk' was a White person. Later, adopted by White Australians, it came to mean an effeminate man. Which is in the same general area as our American 'wonk', sitting in the college library contemplating Aubrey Beardsley rather than venturing forth to risk brain damage on the football field. In politics, too, thinkers are rarely as popular as doers.

If 'wonk' is to establish itself in this country, it will have to defeat a native strain. Since the end of World War I it has been common to talk about things being 'wonky', which is to say, faulty, unreliable and unsound. Which is the last thing any 'wonk' wants to be.